Walking
Orkney

Clan Walk Guides

Walking
Orkney

Mary Welsh

maps and illustrations by
Christine Isherwood

First published Westmorland Gazette, 1994 as
Walks in Orkney
Revised edition published by Clan Books, 1999
Reprinted 2003
This new re-titled edition published by Clan Books, 2007

ISBN-10 1 873597 29 0
ISBN-13 978 1 873597 29 3

Clan Books
Clandon House
The Cross, Doune
Perthshire
FK16 6BE

Printed and bound in Great Britain by
St Edmundsbury Press Ltd, Bury St Edmunds, Suffolk

Foreword

The scale of Orkney lends itself to walking. Driving is a transitory pleasure; an hour will take you to any corner of the 'Mainland'; many islands will not even warm your engine before you run out of road! Walking, on the other hand, slows you down to an island pace and allows the sights and sounds to be appreciated to their fullest. Whether you are planning an imaginary trip back through the centuries to walk through the Neolithic, Pictish or Norse landscapes, or a ramble in search for the plants and birds that make the islands unique, walking is a much more sensible way of enjoying our island heritage.

There is something for every kind of walker in this book – from a short stroll to a day long hike. It provides a range of very varied walks, on both the Mainland and the outer isles, which allow you to explore some of Orkney's most attractive and interesting places. Many of the walks take you along our beautiful and often dramatic coastline; while others wend their way across hill and moorland, or give you an insight to farming life.

Walkers are very welcome in Orkney but, wherever you walk, please remember to act responsibly and follow the Scottish Outdoor Access Code. Take particular care if you have a dog, by keeping it under close control at all times, especially near live- ock and breeding birds.

 Orkney Islands Council is committed to improving outdoor cess in the county and to providing paths for residents and sitors. We hope that you enjoy walking in our beautiful islands th the help of this excellent book.

my Baster
ctor
rtment of Development Services
Islands Council
2005

Acknowledgments

My grateful thanks go to Jane Hannah who helped with the revising of this second edition and helped as my 'Girl Friday'; to VisitScotland for their kind help; to Christine Skene of Orkney Islands Council's Department of Development and Protective Services who gave me considerable help with bringing the book up to date; to Colin Keldie of VisitOrkney who suggested several ideas for extra walks; to Eric Meek and his staff at the RSPB who discussed their reserves with me; to North Link Ferries Ltd for their interest and support; to my husband Tom for his ever-ready support; and, finally to Christine Isherwood, for the illustrations and the cover picture, which so enhance the 40 walks.

Otter

Publisher's Note

This completely new edition of this popular book contains a number of walks from the first edition, which have been thoroughly updated and some routes extended. It contains a considerable number of enjoyable new walks, some more challenging, all delightful. A few have been omitted.

If, in spite of the author's efforts, readers find anything incorrect or misleading in the text we shall be glad to be informed for future reference. However, it must be stated that the book sets out to be an entertaining and helpful guide, and neither the author nor the publishers can be held responsible for any loss or injury that might be considered to result from its use.

The Author's Golden Rules
for Good, Safe Walking

- Wear suitable clothes and take adequate waterproofs.

- Walk in strong footwear; walking boots are advisable.

- Carry the relevant map and know how to use it.

- Take extra food and drink as emergency rations.

- Carry a whistle; remember six long blasts repeated at one minute intervals is the distress signal.

- Do not walk alone, and tell someone where you are going.

- If mist descends, return.

- Keep all dogs under strict control. Observe all 'No Dogs' notices—they are there for very good reasons.

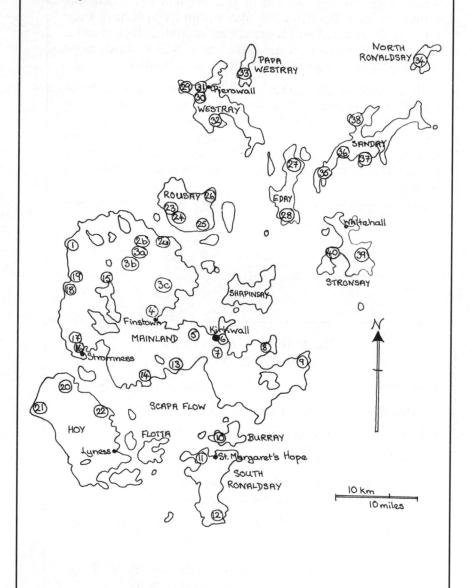

Orkney

Contents

Contents continued page 8

Marwick Head, Birsay Bay, Brough of Birsay and Skipi Geo

Park in the RSPB car park, just above the shore, grid ref 229242. This lies in the north-west corner of Mainland, about 11 miles north of Stromness. It is accessed by leaving the A967 at Twatt and carrying on west down a minor road. At the B9056 turn right and then, almost immediately, take the left turn for the signed car park.

Marwick Head

The Kitchener Memorial on Marwick Head was erected to commemorate Lord Kitchener, Minister of War, and the crew of the HMS Hampshire who died when the boat was sunk by a torpedo on June 5, 1916. Lord Kitchener is best remembered as the face featured on the 'Your Country Needs You' recruiting poster during the 1914–18 war.

The magnificent ruins of the **Earl's Palace, Birsay**, dominate the cottages around it. The notorious Robert Stewart, Earl of Orkney, founded the palace in 1574. It was completed by his even more unpleasant son, Earl Patrick, and consisted of four ranges around an open courtyard, with projecting towers at three of the four corners. The walls have many gun loops and there is a well in the courtyard. Colourful plaques provided by Historic Scotland, in whose care the palace is, show a wealthy man's home and the courtyard as a place of much activity.

Walk 1

On the **Brough of Birsay** you will see evidence of an early Celtic Christian settlement and the much more obvious remains of Norse houses and a 12th century church. The body of St Magnus was buried at Birsay after his murder on the island of Egilsay in 1117 and his body lay either in the church in the village or on the Brough. It was later taken to Kirkwall. The Brough remained a place of pilgrimage until a few centuries ago. *The Brough is a tidal island approached by a causeway that can be crossed only two hours either side of low tide. There are no boat crossings. Tide times are posted in the harbour master's office in Kirkwall.*

1 From the car park, walk north, with Mar Wick Bay to your left, along a gated track that skirts the shore. This is protected from the worst of the sea's force by a buttressed wall and sometimes, after a storm, boulders from the shore and the wall obliterate the path, so be warned. As you go, look back for a good view of the island of Hoy. Carry on where the track becomes grassy, with shallow cliffs immediately to your left. Dawdle on the steadily climbing path to the top of the Head. Take care as you view the sheer cliffs composed of old red sandstone. Many of the ledges are occupied by razorbills, guillemots and fulmars. Close by sit puffins, either alone, or in small groups preening or disappearing into holes in the cliff face to feed their young. There is a constant coming and going of birds as the adults seek food for their chicks, out in the sea beyond the Head, where the waters of the Atlantic and the North Sea mix and teem with fish. The noise, sight, and the smell of so many birds filling the ledges and soaring past is memorable.

2 Continue on to view the Lord Kitchener memorial, then head on the gently descending path towards Birsay Bay. Here look for seals, families of eider, a crowd of shags and listen for the haunting calls of redshanks as they hurry over the shore. Ahead, across the blue waters, you can see the Brough of Birsay and, to the right, you might spot Rousay and the distant cliffs of Westray. Eventually you reach a grassy track, which you follow for a few metres. And then, where it swings right, pass through the fence. Walk diagonally right over the greensward to join a track. Continue ahead and edge an area of exposed sand. Stride on along a track to the road. Turn left and cross the swiftly flowing Burn of Boardhouse on an attractive stone bridge to walk into the village of Birsay to visit the Earl's Palace and perhaps the church of St Magnus (1760).

3 Return back towards the shore and follow the lane to pass through the car park at the Point of Buckquoy. Drop down the steps to the sand and the rock flags of Brough Sound. Cross the man-made causeway and then climb a ramp on to

Puffins

11

the historic island. Pass through the hand gate behind the small shop and museum and walk beside the fence to a gate (where you are asked to keep all dogs on a lead) and onto the short greensward. The path leads up the slope, where sheep graze, to the foot of the lighthouse (built in 1925). From here there is a spectacular view. Take care as you approach the edge of the high sheer cliffs, which are home to fulmars and puffins.

4 Return across the causeway and follow the signpost for Skipi Geo to walk a wide grassy path. The geo or creek, is a sheltered bay and, with its gently-sloping beach, it forms a natural harbour. It has been used by fishermen since Viking times. Look for the flagged way down to the shore and the pleasingly restored turf-roofed hut, also used by fishermen in the past. Close by the hut are boat-shaped depressions, nousts, where boats were stored.

5 To return, walk back to the Point of Buckquoy car park, then follow the lane to pass between the Earl's Palace and the church. At the end of the A966 carry on ahead to reach the B9056. Turn right and follow the B-road as it turns left. Walk on to take the right turn to Skidge. Walk left here along a narrow lane to pass Marwick House. Beyond stroll right and follow the minor road where it turns left. After a bend, left, go on, right, to come to the edge of Choin. Carry on, left, round the coast retracing your outward route to reach the car park.

Practicals

Type of walk: This is an exhilarating, dramatic walk along a lovely stretch of Orkney's coastline. The return uses quiet lanes and narrow roads, though of course you could always return along your outward cliff walk. Do not attempt this walk in high winds. Children should be under control along the cliffs.

Distance: 9½ miles/15.4 km
Time: 5–6 hours, an all-day expedition
Maps: OS Explorer 463 / Landranger 6

NB Don't forget to take your binoculars.

Sands of Evie and Broch of Gurness

Park in the car park at Evie Sands, grid ref 371265. To access this drive north on the A966. At the village of Evie, which lies to the north-east of Mainland, take a narrow right turn and drive to the end of tarmac. The car park has all the necessary amenities.

Gurness Broch was discovered in 1929 by an Orkney scholar, Robert Rendall. He was sketching, sitting on a mound above the shore, when he lost the leg of his stool in a hole and dug down to reveal a staircase on the west of the broch tower. The thick walled tower, or broch, was probably built in the first century BC for a chieftain. The thickness of the walls and the number of doorways to be passed through indicates the importance of the chief. Around the broch were three lines of defensive ramparts and ditches. The entrance was through a long passage on the eastern side and visitors would have approached by sea. Later, outside the tower and within the inner ditch, was built a village where thirty families might have lived. By this time the broch was no longer of defensive importance but may have been lived in as another dwelling. The village as you look at it is now a ruin. The roofs and the tops of the walls are all gone. Two thousand years

Gurness Broch

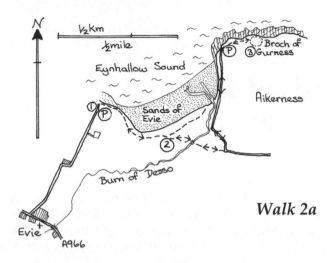

N

½ Km

½ mile

Eynhallow Sound

Broch of Gurness

③

Aikerness

①
P

Sands of Evie

②

Burn of Desso

Walk 2a

Evie

A966

ago this would have been a busy farming settlement with people always wary of competition and sometimes aggressive neighbours. Inside the broch is a well with steps down. Pictish artefacts have been found and also the grave of a wealthy ninth century Norse woman.

1 Return to the tarmac road and walk on along the continuing way, which in summer is bordered with flowers, including the lovely little heartsease. Enjoy the perfect arc of sand where you might spot seals peeping out of the water. Across Eynhallow Sound you can see the shore of the island of Rousay and a similar large broch, Midhowe, see walk 23.

2 At the Y-junction follow the arrow for the Broch of Gurness, taking the right branch, to cross the burn of Desso. Walk on the metalled way to turn left and continue to the official car park, which you pass through to enter the enclosure in which lies the huge broch. It stands on the tip of

Eider with ducklings

14

the Aikerness promontory and is in the care of Historic Scotland. There is a museum and a small entrance fee.

3 Return by your outward route where you might like to spend some time on the lovely sands before returning to where you have parked.

Common seals

<hr />

Practicals

Type of walk: A delightful short stroll to a magnificent archaeological site.

Distance: 2½ miles/4km
Time: 1 hour walking time. Add on time spent at Gurness
Terrain: Easy walking
Maps: OS Explorer 463 / Landranger 6

2b

RSPB Burgar Hill
Bird Hide

Park in the visitor centre car park for the Burgar Hill windfarm, grid ref 344262. This is accessed from the A966 by an unsigned (at the time of writing) left turn, if approaching from Finstown, at grid ref 357266. Turn right after Georth and then take the next left turn to climb to the wind farm.

The RSPB has 13 reserves on the Orkney islands. On small lochans on the hill tops **red-throated divers** nest. These striking birds are known locally as the raingeese; their 'barking' call is supposed to foretell bad weather. They also utter a loud wailing cry, and a gutteral note of alarm. They are birds that are sensitive to disturbance but can safely be viewed from the hide on Burgar Hill. They are graceful, active, playful birds, when on the water. In flight the head is carried a little below the level of the long axis of the body.

Red-throated diver

Walk 2b

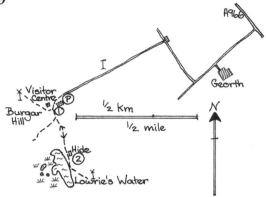

1 From the car park, follow the waymarked track, south, to the hide overlooking Lowrie's Water.

2 Return by the same route.

Practicals

Type of walk: Very short from the car park (300yds/275m), though you might be tempted to walk from the A-road and return by the same route (just under 2 miles).

Time: As much as you can spare.
Maps: OS Explorer 463 / Landranger 6

3a

Mid Hill

Park at the brow of the hill, on the north side of the B9057, 1¼ miles/2km above Evie, grid ref 349246. This can also be accessed by driving the B 9057 for 5½ miles/9km, north-east from Dounby. You can see the trig point on the summit from the parking area, but it is hidden by lesser heights on the way up.

The summit of **Mid Hill** is reached by a rough peat track that climbs steadily from the B-road, over the lonely moorland of the Birsay Moors Nature Reserve.

1 From the marked parking layby, walk west along the B-road for ½ mile to take the peat track, going off right, north. Follow the way, which is quite good underfoot,

Walk 3a

Mid Hill
193m.
Birsay Moors
Nature Reserve
½km
½mile
N
Disused Quarry
B9057

and lined with great banks of heather. Ignore any side turns off the main track. Watch out as you go for hen harriers quartering the moorland. On reaching a flooded section of the path, take to the heather and then return to the track beyond. By now you can see your aim, the trig point on Mid Hill. Remain on the track, which brings you to its base, a wild lonely place with great views – when you peep round some of the high peat hags.

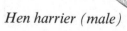

Hen harrier (male)

18

2 Below the trig point, which is set on a high boulder, confusing peat tracks go off in all directions, most ending by the last section to be cut. The Orkney Islands Council Department of Development and Planning are hoping, in the future, to waymark a continuing route that will take you down over the moors and through pastures to the B-road below Skelday Hill. But until then it is better to return by the same route.

Tormentil

Practicals

Type of walk: A fairly easy walk along a track through lonely moorland.

Distance: 2½ miles/4km
Time: 1½ hours
Maps: OS Explorer 463 / Landranger 6

3b

Dounby Click Mill

Before you leave this area, visit Dounby's wonderful little click mill. From the parking area for Mid Hill, drive on west along the B9057 for 1¾ miles/3km. Continue along the B-road where it swings left for another ½ mile. Park on the left, in a widening of the road, beside the sign for the mill, grid ref 323229.

Dounby Click Mill

Walk 3b

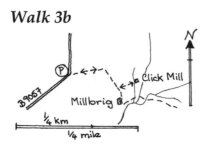

The 19th century **Dounby click mill** used a horizontal waterwheel to drive the mill-stones, which were enclosed in a wooden casing. The bere barley was tipped into a hopper and then it flowed into a hole in the centre of the upper stone. A wooden tongue kept the grain moving, and as it struck a stone projection on the top of the upper stone it made a distinctive 'click, click'. This mill would have served four households. It is housed in a roughly rectangular building constructed of dry flagstones. The roof consists of thin flagstones resting on wooden rafters, with a covering of live turf to keep out the wind.

From the road follow the grassy track to a kissing gate. Beyond, head across the pasture to pass through another. Walk round the fence to find the entrance to the little mill and go inside. Then walk round the outside to see to see the mill wheel in the lower section.

Practicals

Type of walk: A short easy stroll.

Distance: ½ mile/1km
Time: ½ hour
Maps: OS Explorer 463 / Landranger 6

3c

Cottascarth RSPB Hide

Park at the end of the metalled track, just beyond the farmhouse, and signed with a large P at grid ref 368195. There is an information board here about the RSPB reserve. This is a working farm and you should not obstruct any farm vehicles. To access this after visiting the click mill, return along the B 9057 to the A966 and turn right. After 5½ miles/9km, take the right turn for Netherhouse and then another, signposted Cottascarth, to drive the metalled way.

Cottascarth has been called a **'tree-less woodland'**; the natural vegetation of the area was once scrub woodland, which has largely disappeared, leaving only woodland floor plants, such as great woodrush. Cottascarth is the southern portion of the Birsay Moors RSPB reserve. There is access at all times and you are asked not to cause disturbance to nesting birds. The simple hide was erected in 1993 in place of a tiny hide (5m by 5m) erected more than twenty years earlier by Eddie Balfour. Balfour's hide has been re-erected in the Rendall Hills by a keen bird watcher.

Great Woodrush

1 Walk ahead from the information board to take the track marked 'hide'. Go through a gate on the left, then continue. Stride the gradually climbing fenced track, leaving all gates as you find them. Away to the right stand several short, twisted larch and clumps of gorse. Look for green plovers, oyster catchers and hoodie crows. Keep left of the wire fence (arrowed) and turn right at the next arrow across wet rough pasture to the hide, which lies beyond the derelict Dale mill and its surprisingly large sycamore. The hide lies just beyond it.

Short-eared owl

2 The brown wooden hide is a sturdy comfortable hut measuring 12m by 8m and it provides a welcome shelter from which to observe hen harriers, short-eared owls, snipe, arctic skuas, meadow pipits and stonechats. Sheep take refuge below it in rough weather. Spend as much time as you can spare and then return by the same route to rejoin your car.

Dale of Cottascarth
Burn of Dale
② a Hide
Blubbersdale
½ km
½ mile
N
Ⓟ
Lower Cottascarth
Upper Cottascarth
Lettaly
Settiscarth
Midhouse
Netherhouse

Walk 3c

Practicals

Type of walk: Short waymarked route to a bird hide, from where there is interesting viewing

Distance: 1 mile/1.5km
Time: As much time as you can spare
Terrain: Easy walking for most of the way. The track becomes wet towards the end, and the rough pasture in front of the hide can be wet.
Maps: OS Explorer 463 / Landranger 6

4

The Ouse and Binscarth Wood

Park in the well signed car park on the shore of the Bay of Firth, Finstown, where there are toilets, grid ref 362137. Finstown lies 6¾ miles/11km west of Kirkwall.

The Ouse, a saline lagoon, is a shallow arm of the sea at high tide and a stretch of sand and mud at low water. Around the shore thrives sea aster and glasswort. For centuries seaweed, Irish moss, carragheen and dulce were collected from here to feed humans, cattle and sheep. This little walk around the Ouse is a LOW tide walk.

Binscarth Wood

Binscarth Woods were planted in the nineteenth century and extend for seven and half acres. As you walk the track, or the little paths, you will see sycamore, ash, beech, hawthorn, hazel and larch. Once on the track to Binscarth House the shrubby trees almost form a canopy overhead as a result of the prevailing south-westerly winds. The House sits on the hill above the woodland. It was built in 1850 for Robert Scarth, factor for several large estates in Orkney. This is one of the few areas of woodland in Orkney and it provides nesting sites and sanctuary for birds on an island with virtually no hedges and few trees.

Millquoy corn mill, passed on this walk, has a wooden ventilator on the roof constucted for a later drying kiln built alongside the original mill.

1 Walk west, with the sea to the right, and turn right onto the A966. Go on to cross the bridge over the sea inlet and leave the road by a path on the left. The way soon winds left to cross some long sturdy walkways and little footbridges, often passing through yellow irises. Birdwatchers will want to pause here to watch the swans, gulls, redshanks and dunlin. Carry on the delightful way to join a narrow road.

2 Walk on along the road to come to the picturesque Millquoy corn mill, now beginning to deteriorate, with only half of the waterwheel visible and that in poor condition. Wind left and climb up to the main road (A965) and turn right.

Walk 4

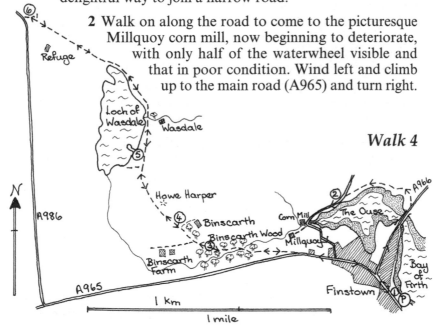

N

A986

A965

1 Km

1 mile

Refuge

Loch of Waedale

Wasdale

Howe Harper

Binscarth

Binscarth Wood

Binscarth Farm

Corn Mill

Millquoy

The Ouse

A966

Bay of Firth

Finstown

Heron

Walk on along the pavement and the verge for 250yds/230m to go through a kissing gate, on the right, signposted 'Footpath to Refuge Corner'. Carry on in the same general direction along a grassy terrace towards the wood. Pass through a kissing gate and stroll down the track, passing below deciduous trees, which support a large rookery. You might also spot a heron's nest. To the left of the track, gap stiles give access to narrow paths through the trees beside the stream that feeds into the Ouse. If the paths are dry you can stroll upstream and then exit onto the track higher up.

3 In July the woodland is carpeted with the pretty pink purslane, which replaces the bluebells in spring time. Walk on uphill, through great bushes of salmon berry. Continue through a small larch plantation and then through another kissing gate onto a stony track, the access track to the fine, sturdy Binscarth House, the latter standing on a hill to your right. Ignore the track descending left to Binscarth farm and carry on with wind-sculptured trees on both sides. Where this access track swings right, walk ahead along the easy-to-miss grassy track.

4 From here look left to see the farm buildings below with their bright blue turrets. The way now passes out into more open countryside, with the slopes to your right covered with gorse. Look here for a man-made mound, which is believed to be a tumulus, possibly a small burial cairn, named Howe Harper on the map. Follow the delightful path, in summer, through a colourful array of wild flowers to a metal gate. Beyond lies the Loch of Wasdale.

5 Dawdle along the loch side, the home to a variety of wetland birds, and then carry on where in summer the marshland is ablaze with ragged robin. Bog cotton grows in profusion and

there is a huge clump of water avens. And then Refuge Corner, named after a nearby house, is reached.

6 You could return from here by road, by turning left twice, but it is much more pleasant to walk back along the track and then, after passing through the kissing gate to the A-road, continuing ahead into Finstown and the sandy parking area.

Ragged Robin, Water avens and Spearwort

Practicals

Type of walk: A pleasing walk around the Ouse, then a relatively sheltered stroll through woods and then, beyond, across moorland. The walk requires stout shoes or boots. If it is high tide when you reach the Ouse, start the walk from the kissing gate on the A-road.

Distance:	5½ miles/9km
Time:	3–4 hours
Maps:	OS Explorer 463 / Landranger 6

5

Wideford Hill and Cairn from Kirkwall

Park at the Pickaquoy Leisure Centre, Kirkwall, grid ref 441109.

Wideford Hill cairn is a communal tomb, dating back to about 3000BC. It is built on an artificially-levelled platform dug into the hillside. Though a torch is provided to enter the tomb, sometimes the battery is flat. Better to take your own. If you do use the torch you are asked to return it and to remember to close the trap door.

1 Leave the parking area by the back left corner and join Muddisdale Road. Walk right and carry on to a junction with a 'dead end' road. Go ahead, uphill, with a house to the left and a fence to your right, beyond which you can see the rugger and football pitches of the leisure centre, away to your right. Then take, on your left, the entrance to the Muddisdale Walk. Keep on the main path as it goes through a pasture where trees, still in their protective sleeves, have been planted.

Wideford cairn

28

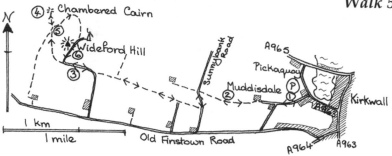

2 Continue on a pleasing walled track beside the golf course, where you are asked to be wary of straying balls. Carry on up the delightful way to the Old Finstown road. Turn left and walk for 200yds/175m. Then cross and take a pleasing farm track that climbs steadily upwards, through pastures, to join the 'new road' to Wideford Hill.

3 Pass a small parking area and carry on until you reach a board, directing you, left, off the road and on along a narrow reinforced peaty path, signed 'Wideford Cairn'. The path winds steadily and diagonally downhill through extensive banks of heather for just over half a mile to come to a gate. Beside it is an arrowed post, marked 'cairn' , directing you on downhill. Continue until you reach the cairn.

4 Take the torch housed in a box and climb the mound to a sliding trap door. At the time of writing it took two of us to open it. You may wish to descend the metal ladder into a rectangular stone chamber, large enough to stand up in. It has three cells leading from it. Heavy lintels are positioned over the cells and the passage. The latter would have been the original very narrow entrance but is not for public use. Ponder on the achievement of the people who, so long ago, created this impressive structure without the equipment we have today. Return to the gate and go through and turn left.

Hooded crow

29

5 Strike ahead on a diagonal sunken peaty track that climbs steadily upwards. After ½ mile look for an indistinct junction of paths and bear acute right up through the heather to a derelict hut. Here join a reinforced track and walk along it for a short way to join the 'new road'. Carry on right along this to the summit, sadly but necessarily clad with transmitting stations. At the highest point look right to see a 'modern' cairn and toposcope to enjoy the magnificent 360 degrees view.

6 Return to the 'new road' and begin your descent. Don't miss the farm track to the left of the road. Follow this to the old Finstown Road. Turn left and then take the signposted footpath, right, beside the golf course and descend to Kirkwall.

Heather

Practicals

Type of walk: A great walk from Kirkwall to the summit of its nearest hill.

Distance: 6 miles/9.8km
Time: 3 hours
Maps: OS Explorers 461 and 463 / Landranger 6

Kirkwall via Seatter to Berstane Road Bridlepath

Park near to the harbour, where there are several car parks, grid ref 449113.

From sections of this walk you can glimpse Kirkwall's **St Magnus Cathedral**. In the early 12th century Orkney was ruled jointly by two earls. In 1115AD the much respected Earl Magnus Erlendsson was murdered on the order of his jealous cousin Earl Haakon. Soon after his burial in Birsay (see walk 1) Magnus's grave was reported to possess healing powers and pilgrims from as far as Shetland came to pray at his shrine. In 1135 he was canonised. In 1137 work began on St Magnus Cathedral by his nephew in which his uncle's relics could lie in splendour.

1 From the harbour walk east along the busy and interesting waterfront. Follow Shore Street and then stride on the continuing Cromwell Road, with a good view of Kirkwall Bay. Carry on through the outskirts of the town and into more rural surrounds. Then

St Magnus Cathedral, Kirwall

31

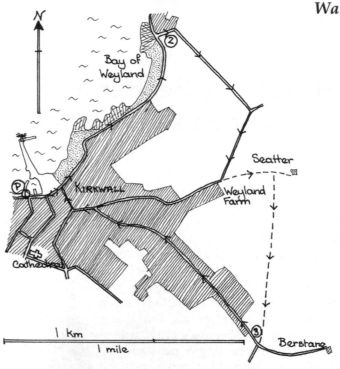

stride the wide grassy area with seats overlooking the Bay of Weyland, where curlews and redshanks probe for prey.

Redshank

2 Follow the road as it swings right and inland. At the T-junction bear right. As you near Weyland Farm, with its tall silo, turn sharp left to walk a reinforced track that leads to Seatter farm. Just before the dwelling take the track on the right, signposted Berstane Road bridlepath. Pass through a gate and stride on. To the left is a wind-bent hawthorn hedge. Beyond the next gate the wide, grassy way is a joy to walk. The hawthorn hedge is now to your right. To the left lies the pleasing Bay of Berstane in Inganess Bay. Look to see the Head of Work, the Head of Holland and Yinstay Head stretching out into the silvery sea like the fingers of a hand. Stroll on, where in summer, pink purslane grows beneath willow, to the signposted exit to Berstane Road.

3 Turn right and continue down the road. Look for a fine sighting of St Magnus's cathedral and of Wideford Hill (walk 5), with Kirkwall harbour soon coming into view. Turn left into East Road and then right into St Catherine's Place and continue to the harbour side.

Pink purslane

Practicals

Type of walk: This is an easy stroll starting from Kirkwall. It is partly urban and partly rural, with pleasing views for much of the way

Distance: 4 miles/6.5km
Time: 1½–2 hours
Maps: OS Explorer 461 / Landranger 6

7

Scapa Pier and the Sand of Wideford

Park near the disused quarry, grid ref 457088. To access this, leave Kirkwall by the A960, and ascend the hill out of the town. Follow the road as it bends right and shortly turn right into a narrow unmarked lane.

This pleasing walk, in summer, is a floral delight. Look as you go for common mallow, tormentil, bedstraw, pink campion, pink clover and vetch. Yellow flags, wild watercress and milkmaids brighten the wet areas on either side of tracks. Gorse, frequently in bloom, adds brilliance to the colourful way. There is much bird life to be seen, such as oystercatchers and hoodie crows that favour the fence posts, curlews and green plover that rise from the fields, redshanks that feed on the shoreline and mergansers which snooze on the still waters of the bay.

Drystone bridge near shore

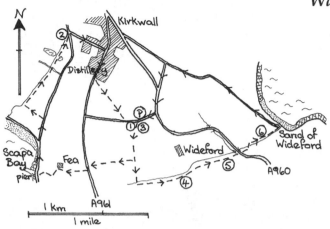

1 Pass through a gate and stride left on the pleasing way in the direction of Caldwell Cottage. Continue along the gated track for just under ½ mile/0.6km and then turn right. Carry on to a kissing gate and the A961. Cross and turn left for 20m to turn right to walk the lane towards Fea. From here you can see Scapa Bay and the brightly-coloured large boats which bring in gas, oil and petrol to its pier. Carry on through the farm, with buildings to the right and bungalows to the left and drop down the continuing way. The track ends at the shore road. Here, at the time of writing you walk right along the B9148 for ¾ mile but, by 2006, Orkney Island Council is hoping to put in an off-road route, see the accompanying map.

2 Then take the right turn (A963) to climb the steep hill. At the top, bear right along the A961. Ahead is the Highland Park distillery, with its pagoda-like chimneys, below which peat fires dry the malt. Follow the A-road with the buildings on either side. After the last distillery building, on the left, cross the road and take the track which goes off, left, to walk a walled way. Where the track swings left, walk

Eider

35

straight ahead along the grassy way. On
reaching the tarmacked road, walk left.
If you wish to finish the walk here
continue on to return to your
car.

3 To continue on this
   'coast to coast' route,
   turn right to stride
   again the access track
   to Caldwell Cottage.
   Walk on the wide
   grassy track. Ignore
   the right turn taken
   earlier and continue
   on a narrower fenced
   way. Cross the duck-
   boarding at the end
   of the track and look
   for the on-going nar-
   row path. This passes
   through lush vegeta-
   tion and comes to the side

Rowan

of the Burn of Wideford. Walk downstream for a few metres to
a footbridge to cross to the opposite bank. Bear left past a waymarked post almost obscured in summer by a wealth of flowers.
Continue on beside a fence on your right and, after crossing two
small ditches, go over a stile. Ahead is a pleasing view of the
lovely Wideford valley, with a small glimpse of the sea beyond.

4 Carry on beside the little burn to the next stile, waymarked, just
   above a ford. Stroll on and follow the path to straddle the next
   waymarked stile and walk below Wideford farm with its long
   roofed barn. It was from here, in 1934, that a Captain Fresson
   flew, establishing the first internal airmail service in Britain. Go
   on through willow, alder and rowan. Keep well up the slope to
   reach the next stile. Beyond, continue on through thick willow
   scrub and, on reaching a fence, climb up beside it to another
   waymarked stile.

5 Stride on to a large clump of willows about the stream. Arrows
   direct you right, beside a fence on your left, to a gate to a track,

36

and on to the A-road, which you cross. Climb the waymarked stile, opposite, with the burn still to your left. Walk on towards a footbridge, which you cross to continue downstream climbing a series of stiles over fences.

6 Head on to pass a lagoon on your left. Then walk left to a footbridge and carry on over the next few metres to another stile and onto a tarmacked track running above the Sand of Wideford. Look right to see a charming two-arched bridge over a small burn near the picnic site. Here you will want to pause on the sands and perhaps picnic here. Then go on to climb the hill, past the wind turbine, the cottage of Heatherquoy and then Inganess farm. Continue on by Quoydandy farm. Stroll on to take the next left turn and walk to the A960, where you turn left. After 250m cross to take the narrow road to rejoin your car.

Curlew

Practicals

Type of walk: This pleasing ramble can be completed as two short walks or as a longer one, crossing the slopes from Scapa to Inganess Bay.

Distance:	3½ miles/5.8km or 7½ miles/12km
Time:	1½ hours or 3 hours
Maps:	OS Explorer 461 / Landranger 6

8

Rerwick Head

Park in a layby close to Rerwick farm, grid ref 539116. To access this, leave Kirkwall by the A960 and continue past the airport. Take the next left turn, signposted Tankerness, and continue to its end.

This glorious headland juts out into the **Wide Firth**, separating Inganess Bay from Deer Sound. The magnificent cliffs are com-

Rerwick Head

posed of innumerable layers of sandstone flags
stacked one on top of the next. Some of
the shoreline flagstones seem large
enough and flat enough on
which to play tennis.

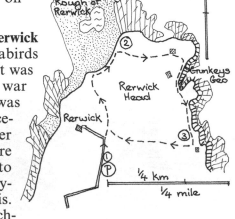

Today all is quiet on **Rerwick
Head**, except for the seabirds
and the crashing waves! It was
not so in the 1939–45 war
when the Wide Firth was
defended by gun emplace-
ments. Many ships, other
than our own, queued here
waiting to be searched to
ensure they were not carrying supplies for the Nazis.
The Head supported search-
lights, various calibre guns, submarine detection apparatus and
all the men to man these defences. It was a busy place.

1 From the layby pass through a kissing gate to walk the grassy
track that swings left towards the shore. The remains of the
coastal defences stand forlornly
about the headland, over-
looking the channel between
Tankerness and the island of
Shapinsay. Wander round this
glorious coastline. If the tide is
suitable, clamber over the great
sandstone flags. Look for shags
and eiders that might be dozing
on the rugged skerries.

2 Pass a small stack, in summer its
top clad in pink thrift. Walk past
several deep ravines where the
water gurgles peacefully and then
round the fenced Grunkeys Geo.
Peer cautiously into all of them
and notice the fantastic layering
of the sandstone.

Shag

39

3 Just before the last ruined building, follow the grassy track that runs inland. Continue along the reinforced track to the kissing gate to return to the parking layby.

Eiders

Practicals

Type of walk: A short walk, full of interest, just right for an evening stroll.

Distance: ¾ mile/1.4km
Time: 1 hour
Maps: OS Explorer 461 / Landranger 6

9

Brough of Deerness, Mull Head and Covenanters Memorial

The Gloup, Deerness

Park in the well sign-posted Gloup car park, grid ref 590079. This is reached by the A960 from Kirkwall. At Snippigar junction, take the right branch to Skaill. From here go on along the continuing narrow road to the car park at the end.

The rocks of **Mull Head** belong to the Old Red Sandstone period and are over 400 million years old. The cliffs are constantly pounded by the sea, gradually eroding them and exploiting weak lines to form stacks, geos, blowholes and unique caves such as The Gloup. This is a sea cave, which has partially collapsed on the landward side, allowing a superb view down the chasm to the sea.

A signpost directs you to railed steps that lead down a steep cliff side to the rocks below, where a narrow path winds, right, to the start of the very steep slope to the top of the **Brough of Deerness**. Once people climbed on their hands and knees to reach this most holy site. Today the ascent is just as steep narrow, sometimes muddy and very close to a sheer drop. But today's walkers can use the well-housed safety chains to ascend to the plateau-like top of the Brough. Here, look for traces of a tenth century Christian settlement, such as grassed over foundations of many tiny rectangular buildings and the remains of a small stone Norse chapel, with a wooden altar, in a walled enclosure. Graves found of two infants, buried in the Christian manner, date from this period. The Brough was a place of pilgrimage from around 1642 to 1860. It was once connected to the mainland by a land bridge. It is a great place to visit but it is accessible only by the above route and care should be taken.

Mull Head Local Nature Reserve extends for about 400 acres of sea cliffs, maritime heath and grassland. It was designated as a reserve by Orkney Islands council in 1993, because of its ecological, archaelogical and geological interest. It is a joy to walk.

Covenanters' Memorial The panel on the memorial tells of the Covenanters who were taken prisoner at Bothwell Bridge and sent for transportation. They perished by shipwreck north–east of the memorial in December 1679 when the overcrowded *Crown* foundered in a storm. The Covenanters, in return for military aid to Charles II, were allowed to introduce their form of worship into England. Later the king reneged on the agreement and the covenanters were savagely persecuted. At the battle on the banks of the Clyde, those prisoners who refused to submit to the king were to be transported. Two hundred and fifty-seven manacled men were taken to Leith docks and loaded onto the ship, which then sailed round the north of Scotland to avoid any rescue attempts. As it entered Deer Sound a gale blew up. A party went ashore for water and was advised by local people to take shelter but the captain paid no heed and sailed on. The storm forced the ship onto rocks at Scarba Taing, 300m north-east of the monu-

Walk 9

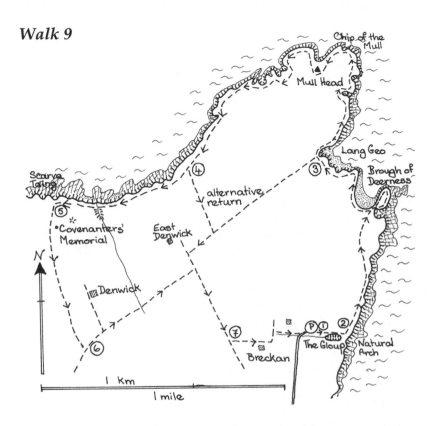

Chip of the Mull

Mull Head

Lang Geo

Brough of Deerness

Scarva Taing

alternative return

⑤

⑥

*Covenanters'
Memorial

East
Denwick

Denwick

④

③

N

⑦

Breckan

The Gloup

Natural
Arch

1 Km

1 mile

ment. The captain refused to allow the prisoners to be released from the hold, though the master is said to have passed a key to the men and some 40 or 50 escaped. Those who floated in on wreckage were forced back into the sea under orders from the captain and many drowned.

1 From the car park take the signposted reinforced path for The Gloup. To the right is a fine view of Copinsay, with its lighthouse, and the cliffs of Deerness. Stand on the viewing bridge to look down into the sea cave. Carry on along the side of the great chasm and stand on the next viewing bridge to look towards the landward end of the cave where a white-topped stream tumbles into the depths.

2 Beyond, follow the signpost directing you along a good path and walk on until you reach the signpost for the Brough of Deerness. After your visit, or if you prefer just to look, carry on to a kissing

43

gate, with an arrow directing you ahead. Wind round a magnificent bay, where in spring, sea birds constantly fly in and out to their nest sites. Go through the next gate and turn right. Here take notice of the warning of the dangerous cliffs around the Lang Geo.

3 Carry on along the path that winds round the Chip of Mull, with its dramatic seascape. Then follow a narrow path, left, to reach the trig point (48m). Another narrow path leads you back to the grassy main path which descends gently, through heather. The heather is then left behind as you stroll on through grassland, stepping over little wet patches, where tiny streams trickle seawards. Continue on round a huge bay to come to a footbridge and a signpost.

4 Here you have a choice of turning left to return on the signed way to the car park; or you can carry on along the cliffs to the monument. This walk continues on ahead along the outside of the fencing to descend steps to cross a footbridge over a grassy gorge. More steps return you to the cliff-top path. Carry on to cross the next bridge and then on reaching the next footbridge the approach is by rougher steps that require care. There is a steep flight of steps to ascend to regain the cliff path. Then the cliffs become lower with the path still remaining outside the fencing.

5 Follow the path as it winds inland. Just below is Scarva Taing where the *Crown* was wrecked. Go through the gate to the foot of the towering monument where you might like to take a short break! Leave by the gate and follow the fenced grassy track as it winds left. At the minor road, turn left to face a gate to Denwick farm. Take note of the arrow on the gate post, which directs you,

right, to a grassy track. This sometimes muddy way runs parallel with the farm's private access road, which should now be on your left. It continues beside the fence on your right, where there is a narrow strip of dry ground and is signposted at the start 'Mull Head and Gloup'.

6 Carry on along the track. Ignore the first right turn and continue on. Just before it reaches a red gate the track becomes very wet. Here take the little path along the banking. At the gate you are parallel with derelict East Denwick. Turn right along a delightful narrow grassy track. This is part of the track walked by those walkers who do not continue to the monument.

7 Follow the track where it winds left and passes to the left of Breckan farm. Descend a few steps more to take a red gate. Beyond, walk the short grassy track and then wind right to return to your car.

Kittiwake

Practicals

Type of walk: This is a glorious challenging walk, which will probably take all day. In summer the route passes through a marvellous carpet of wild flowers.

Distance:	Full walk 6 miles/9.8km. Shorter walk 4¾ miles/7.8km
Time:	4–5 hours and 3–4 hours
Maps:	OS Explorer 461 / Landranger 6

10

Italian Chapel, Burray and Hunda

Use the car park just in front of the Italian Chapel on Lamb Holm, grid ref 485005. This is accessed from Kirkwall by the A961. Cross Churchill Barrier No 1 and the chapel lies to your left.

For the walk from the village of Burray, park by its pier at grid ref 473955. To access this, continue on the A961 to cross the Churchill Barrier 2 to Glimps Holm and then on over barrier 3 to Burray.

The Italian Chapel

The four **Churchill Barriers** link the Orkney mainland with the islands of Lamb Holm, Glimps Holm, Burray and South Ronaldsay. They were created to seal the gaps between the islands and to protect Scapa Flow, a great natural harbour for Allied ships throughout both the 1914–18 war and the 1939–45 war. They were mainly constructed by Italian prisoners-of-war. In October 1939 a German U-boat managed to enter Scapa Flow through Holm and Kirk Sound and torpedoed HMS *Royal Oak*, which sank in 15 minutes, with the loss of 833 lives. The U-boat had manoeuvred between some 20 blockships, deliberately sunk to protect these eastern channels. It took this tragedy to persuade the First Lord of the Admiralty, Winston Churchill, that blockships alone were insufficient to protect the eastern approaches to Scapa Flow and the construction of the barriers began.

The Italian Chapel stands a poignant memorial to 550 prisoners captured during the North Africa campaign. Domenico Chiochetti, with the help of fellow prisoners, transformed two corrugated-iron nissen huts into a beautiful chapel, which all will want to visit. In 1960 Chiochetti returned to help restore the paintwork of the interior.

The causeway that links the island of Hunda with Burray was partly constructed by the army, during the 1939–45 war, using clay quarried from Hunda. It stands on **Hunda Reef** and was finally completed by Balfour Beatty. At either end you might see and hear innumerable seals quietly singing as they sunbathe. As you cross the wide straight way, enjoy the seaweed garden on either side.

Walk 10

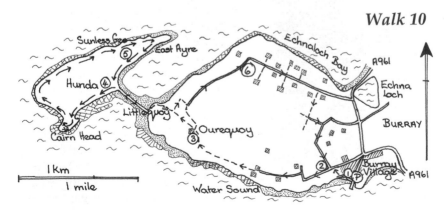

47

1 After visiting the Italian Chapel, drive on across barriers 2 and 3, to park at the pier at Burray village, a small herring station at the end of the 19th century. Sadly barrier 4 has effectively cut off Burray's and St Mary's Hope's fishing boat access to the open sea. Walk back past the boatyard and along the road as it swings right, inland. Turn left along the reinforced track, with Water Sound to your left and picturesque cottages to your right. Turn right at the tarmac turning area and go across the green area seen between two cottages. Climb the slope to a paved gap in the boundary wall and continue to the road, where you turn left to walk the narrow way.

2 Where the latter swings right, carry on ahead. Follow it as it makes a dog-leg turn, swinging right and then left. The traffic-free road takes you between fields of hay, and pastures with cattle. Enjoy the view across the Sound to St Margaret's Hope, another old herring station. Then the island of Hoy comes into view. Where the road ends, continue on along the gated bridle-way, which can be muddy after rain. From here the island of Hunda is soon seen. Beyond the next gate, the grassy track, much drier, crosses a wide greensward that sweeps down to the sea. Flotta, Farra and Cava lie across Scapa Flow.

3 At Ourequoy, stride ahead between two barns. Walk the grassy track, with a fence to your left, passing through two gates

Great skua

to Littlequoy. The track brings you to the yard of the farm, where live George Rouse and Stephanie Jaeger, the owners of Hunda island. Please ask for permission to visit. Stephanie is delighted to welcome you to her showroom and to view her fine knitwear. Follow the track from the farm to cross the causeway.

4 Once on the island take a left hand turn, inside the first fence, and then continue along a sheep trod. The cliffs, the boulders and the shore area are a glorious flower garden in summer. Look across to the south to see the mountains of Caithness, a grey smudge on the horizon. Go on past a ruined broch before continuing round The Hope. Then the Mainland and Kirkwall come into view. Take care on the steeper cliffs. Pass the Sunless Geo, where roseroot and thrift grow on the ledges of the cliffs. As you walk on, a Churchill Barrier comes into view. At East Ayre the narrow trod winds south and you can see Hunda causeway once more.

Roseroot

5 From now on the indistinct path becomes rather boggy, so pick your way with care. Cross the causeway and then follow the track to return through the farmyard. Beyond, take the access track, left and then right, to join the metalled road. Walk left on the road to climb the hill and pause at the top to enjoy the magnificent view back over Hunda and beyond.

6 Carry on along the minor road, past the dwellings Heather Hill, Heather Hall and Klondyke. From this narrow road you can see Echnaloch, separated from the sea by an ayre, over which the road runs. Turn right opposite a house named Newhouse to walk the steadily ascending bridleway. Turn left and stroll to the end of the track, where you carry on right to begin the descent towards Burray village. At the T-junction, walk left and continue through the village to the pier car park.

Practicals

Type of walk: This is a quiet delightful walk, with good views.

Distance: 7 miles/11.4km
Time: 3 hours
Maps: OS Explorer 461 / Landranger 7

11

St Margaret's Hope and Hoxa Head, South Ronaldsay

Park in a layby close to the turning point, grid ref 431940. To access this, cross Churchill Barrier No 4 and continue on the A961. Leave it by the B9403 to drive through the village of St Margaret's Hope. Where the B-road turns left, keep straight on for a short distance, then turn left for Bellevue, and drive on to the parking area at the end of the road.

The village, **St Margaret's Hope**, is named after an early saint, Margaret, a seven-year old princess from Norway. She died here in 1290, while on her way to marry the Prince of Wales, son of Edward I of England. The picturesque village nestles round a sheltered harbour and there is a busy small pier.

Walk 11

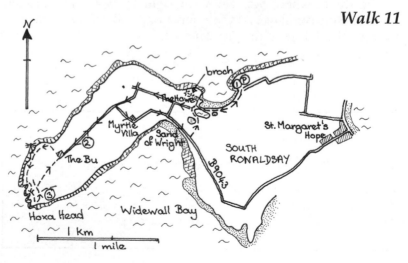

*Gun emplacement,
Hoxa Head*

Hoxa Head has a commanding position high over the Sound of Hoxa, the main entrance to Scapa Flow. The Flow has sheltered ships since traders first visited the islands of Orkney, over a thousand years ago. In both the 1939–45 war and the 1914–18 war the anchorage was a vital facility in the sea battles of the North Atlantic.

The **Balfour Battery** dates from 1940 and formed the first line in the defence of Scapa Flow. On this walk the many concrete buildings and bunkers, which straggle along the highest point of the headland, were once gun emplacements, searchlight positions and lookout posts.

In the summer, on the **Sand of Wright**, the boys of the area take part in a ploughing match with the same rules as their fathers observe in their matches. In the past the ploughs were quite simple, a cow's hoof on a stick for instance. Today the ploughs are often miniature ones, handed down through the generations. Before the competition takes place the boys, and girls as well, dress up as horses and parade through St Margaret's Hope. The parade has taken place for the last 80 years and some of the beautiful ornamental costumes are handed down through the family.

1 From the parking area, walk down the concrete track towards the shore, and then bear left to walk above the lovely sandy bay,

which is backed by a shingle beach. To the left lies a marsh and next to it is a large lagoon. Behind the lagoon is more marsh. Once these three areas were one. Towards the end of the bay you go by, on the right, a sturdy house, The Howe, and behind it are the remains of a substantial broch. Here, according to the Orkneysaga, was buried in the 10th century, Earl Thorfinn Skull-Splitter. At the footpath sign, turn left and then continue along an unclassified road. At the T-junction continue ahead and walk, for about a mile, the delightful minor road from where there are extensive views over the Sound of Hoxa to Flotta.

2　Go past a signed parking area and walk on to just past The Bu (Norse for the home/farm of the principal landowner). Turn right through a gate and on along a grassy track to pass through two kissing gates. Beyond the second, bear left to walk along the grassy-topped cliffs overlooking the Sound, where in summer scurvy grass grows in profusion and, as its name suggests, was once used for the prevention of scurvy. From here you might spot one or two oil tankers anchored out in Water Sound, waiting to pick up their shipment of oil. Then you begin to pass the fenced ruins of the Balfour Battery. Carry on the narrow path, which comes close to the edge of the very steep cliffs, where the sea savages the rocks far below. Carry on with care. Wind round a railed deep geo and follow the path as it weaves round more geos and eventually comes to a kissing gate.

3　Turn inland to pass through a large area of the foundations and plinths of buildings, which give you an indication of the scale of the military occupation of this site. Beyond, stroll the delightful, fenced, gated, grassy track, which eventually returns you to the Bu. Carry on along the minor road, walked earlier, and after just over half a mile, turn right. Stroll on to turn left after passing Myrtle Villa. At a small junction another right turn brings you to the B9043 that runs just above the lovely white Sand of Wright. After a long pause

Scurvy-grass

here, stand with your back to the bay and take the grassy track to the left of the wire fence on the left side of the excellent facilities – toilets, hot water and soap, waiting room, picnic table and information panel. The track passes between the lagoon and the marshy area. At the shore, turn right to return to where you have parked.

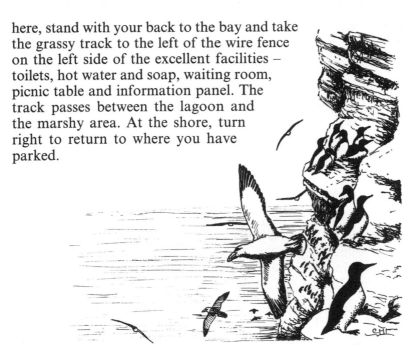

Fulmars and Guillemots

Practicals

Type of walk: This walk is not really suitable for young children as, in places, the path comes near to the edge of dangerous cliffs. Some adults will find it too vertiginous. Those with a turn for military history will love it. The views are incredible, the bird life very active. Not to be attempted on a very windy day.

Distance:	5½ miles/9km
Time:	3–4 hours
Maps:	OS Explorer 461 / Landranger 7

12

Tomb of Eagles,
South Ronaldsay

Park in the large parking area at Liddel farm, grid ref 464839. To access this, take the A961 from Kirkwall almost to its end at the foot of South Ronaldsay. At the T-junction, where A-road turns right for Burwick pier, turn left and follow the signs for the Tomb of Eagles.

The Neolithic chambered tomb, known as the **Tomb of Eagles**, was excavated by the Simison family, on whose land it stands, in 1958, after trying for many years to get the authorities involved. The farmer found the bones of at least 340 people in the tomb plus fish bones, seeds, pottery and the remains of white-tailed eagles. It is believed that the dead were laid outside until the

Tomb of the Eagles

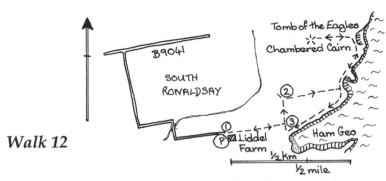

Walk 12

eagles had picked the bones clean before they were laid to rest in the communal tomb. The tomb is thought to have been used from 3500 to 2400BC. After that time the top was taken off and it was deliberately filled in.

1 Visit the small museum where you are given a short lively talk and encouraged to handle skulls, eagle claws, fragments of fascinating pottery, and beads. After being provided with limited wet weather clothing if necessary, you set off along a fenced track to the left of the farm. It brings you to the remains of a Bronze Age dwelling (1500–500BC). Here you are given a fascinating talk and are shown what is believed to be the living quarters with a flagstone floor, a large hearth and the middens. Central to all is a large flagstone trough, bedded in the underlying clay, to which hot stones were continually added to heat the water for cooking food. Again you are encouraged to handle various stone artefacts and to wander around.

2 Then carry on along another fenced track, which brings you to the edge of the cliffs composed of innumerable thin flags of sandstone. Here fulmars nest and the way is a mass of thrift, with roseroot growing in the crevices of the cliff face. The path leads to the chambered tomb. To enter you can crawl on hands and knees, using kneeling pads and hand pads, or lie on a sturdy

Thrift

55

trolley and propel yourself along a low ceilinged passage. At the end is a surprisingly spacious stone chamber with upright slabs of stone providing partitioning. There are several small cells and shelves. Then make your exit and return along the cliff edge, with magnificent views into several geos as you go.

3 Where the fenced track turns right, continue beside the wire fence to walk along the cliffs of the north side of a small bay. Turn right at the end of the bay and then left to walk another grassy track to return to your car.

White-tailed Eagle

Practicals

Type of walk: Short but very interesting.

Distance: 1 mile/1.5km
Time: 2hours
Maps: OS Explorer 461 / Landranger 7

There is a reasonable entrance fee. Usual concessions.

13

RSPB Hobbister nature reserve

First walk: park on the south side of the A964, four miles south-west of Kirkwall, grid ref 395069.

Second walk: park down a signposted side turn, south off the A964, one mile west of the first parking area, grid ref 384065.

The 1,875 acres of **Hobbister reserve** are leased to the RSPB by James Grant & Co, Highland Park Distillery, which retains peat cutting rights.

1 Walk into the reserve from the parking area, along a track through heather moorland. Where the way divides, walk left for a good view of Waulkmill Bay. Take care as you approach the cliffs of Roo Point, where many fulmars nest. Return to the

Walk 13

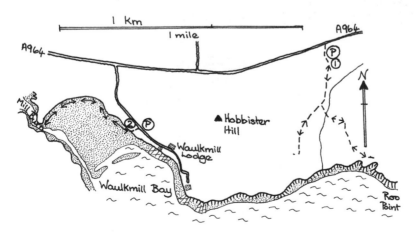

57

Waulkmill Bay

division of the path and take the right fork. In summer, as you walk through the banks of heather, listen for the hum of an immense number of insects. Look for meadow pipits and skylarks flitting about the moorland plants. Where the track swings right, you have reached the end of the right of way and you are asked **not** to continue. As you return to the parking area, you might spot a merlin or a kestrel, or both. Hen harriers nest on the reserve and short-eared owls can be seen. The Orkney vole, which is particularly common, provides plenty of food for these birds-of-prey.

2 From the second parking area, descend steps to the glorious sands of Waulkmill Bay. Carry on, right, along the bay to the estuary of Mill Burn. Here shelduck, arctic tern, redshank,

Orkney vole

oyster-catchers and common gulls feed. The sands are extensive and a delightful place to idle and beachcomb. Return along the shoreline back to the car park.

Merlin

Practicals

Type of walk: Both attractive short walks.

Distance: 1 miles/1.5km and ½ mile/ 1km
Time: 1 hour
Maps: OS Explorer 463 / Landranger 7

14

The Bu and St Nicholas's Church, and The Breck, Orphir

Park at the Orkneyinga Saga Centre, Orphir, grid ref 335045. To access this leave Kirkwall on the A964 and after 8 miles, turn left on the road to Gyre.

The Bu, a manor house of the Norse Earls of Orkney in the 12th century, was built to the north side of the round church. It comprises a group of farm buildings, a drinking hall for feasting and other storerooms and chambers. The stones and foundations you can see, to the left of the path, may have formed part of that complex.

St Nicholas's church, is believed to have been mentioned in the Orkneyinga Saga, composed in 1136. It is thought to have been built by Earl Haakon Paulson to make amends for the murder of Earl Magnus of Egilsay in about 1116. Earl Paulson made a pilgrimage to Jerusalem after the murder and the plan of the church may have been inspired by the Holy Sepulchre.

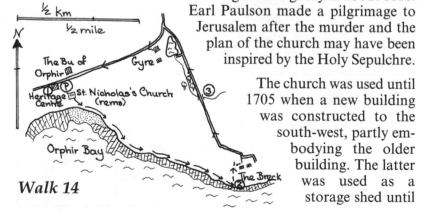

Walk 14

The church was used until 1705 when a new building was constructed to the south-west, partly embodying the older building. The latter was used as a storage shed until

1756 when two-thirds was pulled down to provide stone to repair the later building. This later church has since been demolished and part of the circular wall and the **apse of the old church** has been dramatically revealed.

1 Leave the churchyard by a handgate in the east wall and walk towards the shore. Cross the footbridge over a small burn to a gate. Beyond, stroll along the cliffs overlooking Orphir Bay and Scapa Flow. Then continue with the fence to your left, just above the stony shore, with spectacular views over to Hoy. Beyond the second pasture, the way continues inside the wall where the sea has eroded the cliffs. Press on along the sward of the low cliffs where, in summer, a multitude of flowers colour the way and then through heather, crowberry and low-growing willow to the area known as The Breck.

2 Look here for two stone-built fishermen's huts. Close to the huts

Crowberry

61

is a natural gully that might have been a slipway down to a tiny bay and for hollows (nousts) where boats might have been sheltered. Bear left from here, to follow a narrow path inland, keeping to the right of a small burn. Pass a derelict stone cottage and join an access track, which heads on inland. At the tarmacked road, turn left.

3 Continue uphill to walk beside Gyre burn and then stroll on as the road passes deciduous woodland. Ignore a left turn and stroll on past a small lake, once a mill pond and now colonised by reeds. At the road junction, turn left and walk the quiet narrow road, past Gyre house with its crenellated tower to return to the Orkneyinga Saga Centre.

While in this part of Mainland you might wish to drive towards Stromness to visit the Unstan chambered tomb. It is signposted off the A965 and lies back from the road, behind a dwelling. The stone tomb, which dates from about 3500 to 3000BC, has lost its original roof but inside, reached by a low passage, is a large oval chamber. This is partitioned into five compartments by upright slabs of stone and there is one cell with a sturdy lintel that carries Norse runes and the carving of a bird. During excavation in 1884, the remains of skeletons were found, including two crouched skeletons in the side cell. Pottery found was of the type known as Unstan ware.

Practicals

Type of walk: The centre with its audiovisual display is well worth a visit. Pleasing walking to The Breck.

Distance: 2 miles/3.4km
Time: 2 hours
Maps: OS Explorer 463 / Landranger 7

15

Drover's Road, Swartland to Russland Road

Park at the start of the signposted footpath, near Swartland, grid ref 275209. To reach this, take the narrow road heading west from Dounby.

This inland linear walk, **Swartland Drover's Road**, is two miles long. It runs along part of the old Birsay to Kirkwall road. The track was once used by drovers taking their cattle to market. They had to move the stock slowly, perhaps only a few miles a day, to keep them in prime conditon. Maybe the passing cattle helped the plants beside the track to grow a little better! Swartland corner, where this walk starts, is close to the now abandoned wartime airfield of Skeabrae. There are a few abandoned croft houses and a church in this area, which would have been in use when the road was still travelled.

As this is a linear walk you might wish to arrange to be picked up at the Merkister Hotel or Harray Mill, Russland. You could combine this walk with a visit to the Lochside viewpoint, Maeshowe Cairn, Tormiston Mill, Stones of Stenness and the magnificent Ring of Brodgar. If you do not have transport awaiting you, return by the same route.

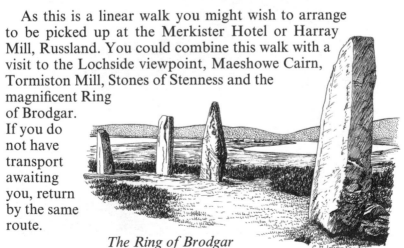

The Ring of Brodgar

The glorious **Loch of Harray** is an SSSI. It supports a wide variety of wetland birds and is home to perhaps the largest collection of mute swans to be found anywhere in Orkney. At the end of the Swartland Drover's Road carry on beside the loch to see the disused Harray Mill. This traditionally built 19th century parish meal mill is peculiar in that before 1875 it did not possess a drying kiln. Farmers wishing to make use of it had to dry their own barley and oats before taking them for milling.

Walk 15

1 Join the wide fenced track, which leads you through the agricultural heart of Orkney. Fields of hay and barley border the way and in pastures beef cattle graze. As you walk, look right to see the dramatic tops of the hills of Hoy and to the left the heather-clad hills of north-east Mainland. Pass through the red-stained kissing gates to reach the B9057, which you cross. To the right stand the Decca pylons, a navigational system for ships.

Mute swans

2 Stride on the continuing track through more quiet pastures. Then the Loch of Harray comes into view. On it shores stands a sewage plant, which uses an innovative technique for disposing of the outfall. It allows it to percolate through the extensive reed beds. Just before the landscaped site, join the reinforced wide track that passes over a narrow fast-flowing stream. Where the reinforced way swings left carry on along the track. When you reach the end of the footpath and bridleway, turn right and walk down the quiet road to Merkister Hotel, once the home of the writer, Eric Linklater. Here you might wish to enjoy a welcome cup of tea etc.,

3 Follow the minor road as it runs beside the lovely loch. Continue on to see the disused Harray Mill.

Meadow Pipit

Practicals

Type of walk: This is a level inland footpath and bridleway taking you the through the peaceful heartland of Mainland.

Distance: 5miles/8.2km if you return along the track.
Time: 1½ hours each way.
Maps: OS Explorer 463 / Landranger 6

16

A Walk through Stromness

Park in the large long-stay car park, at the north end of Stromness, grid ref 255095. This is accessed by the A965.

Stromness stretches along a narrow coastal strip below **Brinkies's Brae**. The single street curves gently along the line of

Stromness

the shore, flanked on both sides by tightly packed stone houses and shops, some three-storeys high. The gable ends of many of these dwellings face the shore, each with a small pier or slipway for trading vessels. Steep alleys lead down to these. Under the streets run secret passages (now blocked) used by smugglers. Buildings were built to withstand the sometimes harsh weather, with small windows set into thick walls. The single street is paved with local flagstones, with cobbling down the middle, all of which blends well with the stonework of the houses.

Stromness is the second biggest town on the Orkney Mainland. It sits on the west side of the natural harbour of Hamnavoe. In the late 18th century the growth of the whaling industry made the town an important last port of call for ships bound for the waters of Greenland.

1 Close to the car park is Speddings, a fine house with two arches in its ground floor and a flight of steps to the main house. Long before the A-road was constructed the tide would have washed the side of the house. It was built by a Lieutenant James Robertson, the commander of HMS Beresford, which attacked an American squadron at the Battle of Plattsburgh in the war of 1812.

2 Stroll on past the Speddings, with the deep-water harbour to your left. Enjoy the activity, as varied and busy today as it has always been. In

¼ km

¼ mile

Walk 16

67

the 18th century, war brought prosperity to the harbour, followed, in the 19th century, by expanding trade, boat-building and repairs, and a herring boom. Stromness was one of the headquarters of the Royal Navy in both world wars. Today roll-on, roll-off ferries come into the harbour.

3 Continue along the waterside to the tourist office, which occupies a crow-stepped gabled house with a slate roof, once a rice warehouse constructed in the 1760s.

4 Walk on into an open area where stands the Alexander Graham fountain. In 1743 he led the legal battle for Stromness to become an independent burgh enabling the town to trade abroad without having to pay a special tax to Kirkwall. During the process he bankrupted himself.

5 Turn right to walk into flagged John Street and then up a sloping alley towards Millar's House. Look for the plaque over the door with the words 'God's providence is my inheritance' and the date 1716. This is the earliest dateable house in Stromness.

6 Return along John Street and wander down Victoria Street, lined with tightly packed houses, many of which are small businesses with shop fronts surviving from years gone by. Between many of the houses narrow alleys lead to small moorings and the alleys give delightful glimpses of the harbour. On the right, cobbled stepped closes lead up the hillside.

7 Pause at the Pier Arts Centre, once the recruiting centre for the Hudson Bay Company. Pass through the arch to see the boat jetty beyond and the extensive view out into the harbour.

8 Wander through the maze of alleys that climb right, opposite the Lounge Bar.

9 Weave left to enter Church Street, aptly named as it has three churches in 200m. Continue into Graham Place, where cobbles run through the middle of large flags. Alexander Graham (see no. 4) lived on the left. A small number of houses were demolished here to help the traffic flow.

10 Beyond Graham Place, walk on through the narrowing main street to see the Kyber Pass, a narrow stepped alley that linked the houses on the banks with the jetties.

11 Carry on to pass the lifeboat station and then a wider area is reached, where Alfred Street joins Dundas Street and Helliehole Road.

12 On the corner of the latter is Stromness library, built in 1905.

13 Look for the large premises that house the Northern Lighthouse depot, once another part of the Hudson Bay Company. Part of the building replicates the living quarters found at the foot of lighthouses.

14 Continue along the attractive Alfred Street to the museum housed in the old town hall. Find time to enjoy the displays. Here much of the life of the Hudson Bay Company's employees is revealed.

15 Follow the quiet way into the older end of the town. Login's well lies to the right. Peer through the glass front to see the plethora of ferns thriving within. This well watered the Hudson Bay Company's ships from 1670 to 1891. Captain Cook's ships, Sir John Franklin's and the merchant vessels of earlier years all used the well. It was sealed in 1931.

16 Head on along the paved way, now South End, which runs into Ness Road. Here the flagstones cease. Sit on Stanger's Brae, beside the cannon, and enjoy the magnificent seascape. The gun was fired on the arrival in the harbour of the ships of the Hudson Bay Company .

17 Look right from here to see a charming house, which looks like two. Here lived a Mrs Christian Robertson, a redoubtable lady who, as shipping agent, employed hundreds of men to sail the whaling boats. Then begin your return through the main street. As you go beware of unexpected traffic along the cobbled and flagged main street.

Practicals

Type of walk: Fascinating small town, not to be missed.

Distance: ½ mile/1km one way.
Time: 2–3 hours
Maps: OS Explorer 463 / Landranger 6

17

Warebeth Beach, Stromness Reservoir and The Loons

Park at the point where the Ness Road, Stromness, turns inland, grid ref 255080.

There are spectacular views over **Hoy Sound** to the islands of Hoy and Graemsay. Strong tides run through the Sound and large standing waves and strong eddies make this a stretch of

Hoy from near Stromness

water not to be taken lightly. This area was important during the 1939–45 war in defence of the Hoy Sound entrance to Scapa Flow.

The gun after which the viewpoint, visited towards the end of the walk, is named was a **32–pounder cannon** mounted there before the 1914–18 war. In 1941 the army removed it to make room for an anti-aircraft gun emplacement to defend Scapa Flow. The cannon was used as scrap to help the war effort.

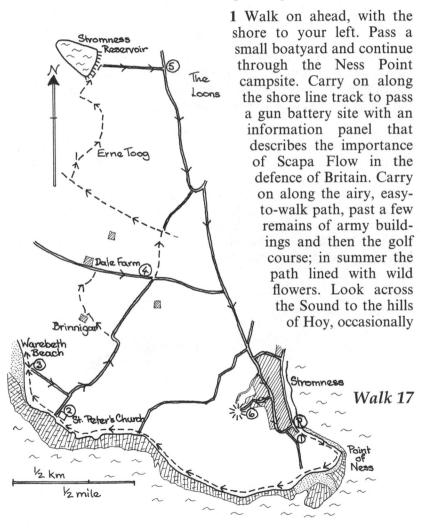

1 Walk on ahead, with the shore to your left. Pass a small boatyard and continue through the Ness Point campsite. Carry on along the shore line track to pass a gun battery site with an information panel that describes the importance of Scapa Flow in the defence of Britain. Carry on along the airy, easy-to-walk path, past a few remains of army buildings and then the golf course; in summer the path lined with wild flowers. Look across the Sound to the hills of Hoy, occasionally

Walk 17

veiled in mist, towering over the low-lying Graemsay island. Peer up Burra Sound between the two islands, where you might spot a boat, carrying amateur divers, circling the blockship *The Inverlaine*. The boat struck a mine in 1941 and was sunk here in 1944. Notice the fine sandstone skerries that tilt out into the sea.

2 Pass through a red kissing gate to wind through St Peter's cemetery and view the ruined church. Many of the graves have magnificent headstones but some of the legends are very sad. Return to the shore and carry on along the narrow path, on the outside of a wire fence, to arrive at Warebeth Beach, probably named after the large quantities of seaweed (or Ware) that gets washed up here. In times past it was a great place for collecting kelp stalks, which were collected and dried for export to extract useful minerals. There are still remains of 'drying dykes' along the top of the beach. A narrow road ends at the beach.

3 Leave the beach and walk, east, along the narrow road, which runs behind the graveyard. Follow it as it climbs gently to bend sharp left and then immediately right. Here turn left to walk a grassy trod to pass to the right of ruined Brinnigar farm. Continue on the winding grassy trod as it bears steadily right to reach Dale Farm and a narrow road. Turn right and walk to a junction of roads. Here look for a dirt track climbing left, just before a bungalow on the left. At the Y-junction take the left branch to walk a reinforced track.

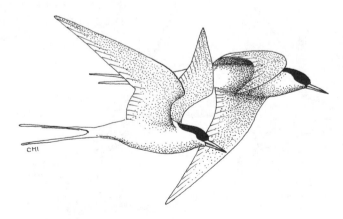

Arctic terns

4 Head on until you have to edge round a spring that forms a large pool across the way. Stroll on and take the track, climbing right, up on to Erne Toog, which in late summer is a mass of purple heather. Press on along the indistinct way, keeping beside the fence on your right. Follow the fence as it winds left, with the small Stromness reservoir coming into view. Keep parallel with the fence as it winds left again and joins the waterworks track. Here turn right and descend with the dam to your left. Wind round right along the now metalled way to reach a road. Ahead lies the RSPB wetland reserve, The Loons, a large boggy area with a myriad of small pools, which much delights a group of terns.

5 Turn right and stride on along below Mewie Hill to arrive at a T-junction. Turn left and almost immediately right to descend. At the next crossroads, go on down a narrower road and turn right to descend the 'main road'. At the next right turn, a no-through-road, signed 'Gun Viewpoint', turn right. Follow the next signed footpath, left, and walk to the large outcrop of rock from which Stromness pilots once watched for boats approaching from the west or east, through the South Isles, to avoid the dangerous tides of the Pentland Firth. The site was also used in both world wars.

6 Return to the 'main road' and go on downhill to where you have parked.

Practicals

Type of walk: Easy walking to the cemetery. Steepish road climb. Delightful walk through the heather to the reservoir. Fine views. More road walking than usual.

Distance:	6½ miles/10.5km
Time:	4 hours
Maps:	OS Explorer 463 / Landranger 6

18

Skara Brae

Park in the spacious parking area in front of the Visitor Centre at Skara Brae, grid ref 236187.

Skara Brae, a small village with houses, workshops and alleyways, throve on the shore of the Bay of Skaill 4,500 years ago. The village gradually became choked by it own rubble and then over the millennia was completely buried under sand blown in from the magnificent bay. In about 1850, a tremendous storm

House at Skara Brae

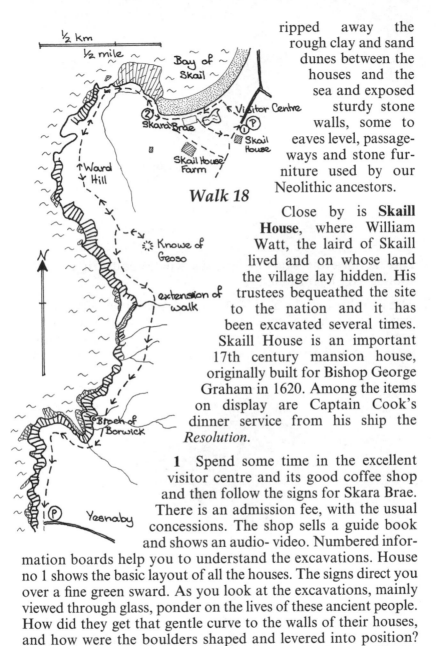

½ km

½ mile

Bay of Skail

Visitor Centre

Skara Brae

Skail House

Skail House Farm

Ward Hill

Walk 18

Knowe of Geoso

extension of walk

Broch of Borwick

Yesnaby

N

ripped away the rough clay and sand dunes between the houses and the sea and exposed sturdy stone walls, some to eaves level, passage-ways and stone fur-niture used by our Neolithic ancestors.

Close by is **Skaill House**, where William Watt, the laird of Skaill lived and on whose land the village lay hidden. His trustees bequeathed the site to the nation and it has been excavated several times. Skaill House is an important 17th century mansion house, originally built for Bishop George Graham in 1620. Among the items on display are Captain Cook's dinner service from his ship the *Resolution*.

1 Spend some time in the excellent visitor centre and its good coffee shop and then follow the signs for Skara Brae. There is an admission fee, with the usual concessions. The shop sells a guide book and shows an audio- video. Numbered infor-mation boards help you to understand the excavations. House no 1 shows the basic layout of all the houses. The signs direct you over a fine green sward. As you look at the excavations, mainly viewed through glass, ponder on the lives of these ancient people. How did they get that gentle curve to the walls of their houses, and how were the boulders shaped and levered into position? Why build at Skara Brae? Perhaps there was a fresh water lagoon close by. Did they get all their protein from the sea in the winter?

Skylark

Did they use the skins of beached whales and driftwood for roofing over their dwellings?

2 Then go through the gate in the far, shore corner of the village and walk on and up along the cliffs. Stroll the path and from the headland look down, with care, to see the Hole o' Row, a natural arch, where the sea has pierced right through the headland.

Corn marigold

Continue on the path over Row Head, Ward Hill and to the cairn, Knowe of Geoso. Pause here to enjoy the superb views and then return by the same route. Leave yourself time for a worth-while visit to the charming Skaill House.

If you are able to be met at Yesnaby car park, continue on along the dramatic cliffs, viewing the many geos as you go, with care, and pausing at the ruined Broch of Borwick, perched on the precipitous headland.

Beached whale

Practicals

Type of walk: Skara Brae is a must. The walk over the cliffs to Yesnaby is most dramatic. Sturdy boots and waterproofs required.

Distance:	To the Knowe of Geoso, 2/½miles / 4km return. To Yesnaby from Skaill Bay 3 miles/5km one way.
Time:	2 hours and 3 hours
Maps:	OS Explorer 463 / Landranger 6

19

Bay of Skaill

Use the parking area opposite the toilet block on the sands of Skaill Bay, grid ref 235193. This lies a few metres north of Skara Brae visitor centre.

This walk starts from the **Bay of Skaill**, where you will want to linger, but rapidly moves inland through the gently undulating countryside. The lovely bay of glorious sand has, since time immemorable, been eroded by the sea and the shore line has steadily receded. Skara Brae would have been constructed well behind a sheltering line of sand dunes.

An **Orkney gate** is constructed of several poles that support rows of barbed wire. They are in use all over Mainland Orkney and the islands where trees and therefore timber is in short

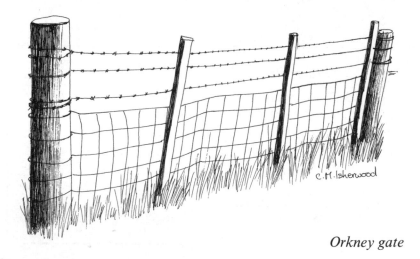

Orkney gate

supply. They are effective and until you 'get your eye in' are not easy to distinguish from the ubiquitous fencing.

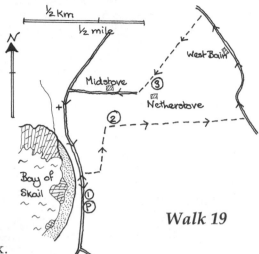

Walk 19

1 Walk on, north, for a few steps to turn right into a pleasing grassy track. When you reach a gate, turn left through an Orkney gate to walk another grassy track. Ragged robin, sea may-weed, yellow flags, bedstraw and corn marigolds flower along the way. In wet areas kingcups and forget-me-nots thrive. Horsetails growing in profusion on either side of the track show how wet it can be.

2 Turn right into the next grassy track, leading off by a stretch of drystone wall, and stride out into the peace of the gently rolling countryside. Stroll on, with fields of barley or hay on either side, until you reach a narrow road, where you turn left. Climb the steadily ascending hill. Ignore a right turn to Housegarth and walk on where, in spring, curlews call from the pastures. Look for Orkney gates that give access to the fields on either side. At the next right turn, for Quoyloo church, turn left to press ahead along one more wide grassy track. Ahead is a magnificent view of the grassy slopes topping the cliffs above Skara Brae. You might also be able to spot the natural arch, Hole

Curlew

79

o' Row, jutting into the sea. Beyond, you can see the sheer rose-pink cliffs of Hoy.

3 When you reach a modern cottage, turn right and walk the narrow, reinforced road to the B9056, where you turn left. On the right stands a disused church. Look in the graveyard for the en-closed graves of William Watt and his family. He was the laird of Skaill on whose land Skara Brae lay hidden.

Ragged robin

Practicals

Type of walk: Short airy stroll through gentle countryside.

Distance:	3 miles/5km
Time:	1–2 hours
Maps:	OS Explorer 463 / Landranger 6

20

North Hoy and the Rackwick footpath

For information on the passenger and cycle service on the m.v Graemsay from Stromness to Moness Pier tel: 01856 850624. For information on the roll-on/roll-off ferry m v Hoy Head, from Houton, in Orphir, to Lyness, tel: 01856 811397. From Lyness drive north to park at the start of the Rackwick footpath, grid ref 223034 and start the walk at point 2, or at the Moness Pier grid ref 246039.

The name **Hoy** means high land. After Mainland, Hoy is Orkney's largest island and it contains magnificent scenery. The north and west of the island are very hilly and the south is low-lying and fertile. Like the rest of Orkney, Hoy is steeped in history. There are sites that date from pre-historic times, through the Viking period and up to the present day. Much of Hoy is composed of Upper rather than Middle Old Red Sandstone that has been weathered into a complex of steep and craggy hills.

Although the present **Hoy Kirk** is only 110 years

Hoy church

81

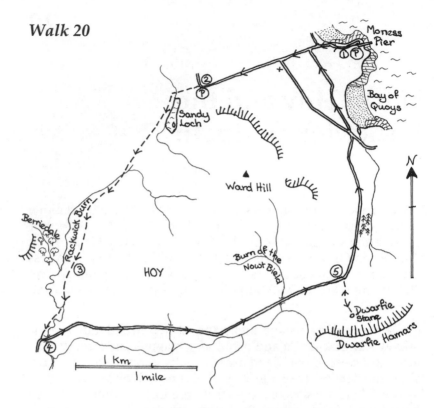

old it has a wooden pulpit from a galleon of the Spanish Armada dated 1624, topped by a simple wooden cross from HMS Vanguard (1914–18 war) created by a marine who made this island his home. The wooden roof and floor provide excellent acoustics for concerts held here.

A solitary block of red sandstone lying below **Dwarfie Hamars**, is a prehistoric tomb with a man-made passage and flanking cells. It is believed to date from about 3000BC. The tomb was formerly sealed by a blocking stone, which now lies in front of the entrance. Look for the interesting graffiti, much of it Victorian. One inscription is in Persian and local people tell of a Major William Mouncy, an eccentric who, after working as a spy in Persia, would dress in Persian costume and sleep in the tomb.

1 Walk up the road from Moness pier (good facilities here) with a dramatic view ahead of Cuilags and Ward Hill. Continue ahead

Meadow pipit

along the narrow road, which in summer is lined with a glorious array of flowers. To the left, high on its hill, stands Hoy Kirk. Stride on and then glance back right to see a conspicuous grassy hill. This is a volcanic plug, a remnant of the lava that once flowed over the landscape.

2 Where the road swings sharp right, continue ahead along the signposted Rackwick footpath. Here in the parking area (maybe used by those who have come by the roll-on roll-off ferry from Lyness pier and who will start their walk from here) an information panel welcomes you to the North Hoy nature reserve. The path is clear to follow and is in good condition. Footbridges and duckboarding conveniently placed and arrowed boulders all assist you to cross the small streams. The way climbs gently and descends gently through the heather moorland of the dramatic U-shaped Rackwick Valley. On the left you pass Sandy Loch, whose dammed waters flow under a sturdy bridge.

3 After a mile and a half, look right for Berriedale Wood, the most northerly natural woodland in Britain. Here grows aspen, rowan, birch and hazel, providing breeding sites for small birds. It is the last remnant of the light scattered woodland common in Orkney when the first settlers arrived about 5500 years ago. Towards the end of the footpath it comes close to the Rackwick Burn, a deeply-stained fast-flowing stream, its banks lined with low-growing willow and a host of water-loving plants. Ahead lies the settlement of Rackwick and the Pentland Firth. Beyond, you can see the Scottish mainland, a smudge of grey on the horizon.

4 Join the narrow road and turn left. Carry on to cross the Burn of the Nowt Bield (burn of no sheepfolds). Look upstream to see an armchair-shaped corrie, scoured out by a retreating glacier. To the right a burn tumbles out of its glen in a series of pretty falls. After two miles, you come to the signpost for the Dwarfie Stane. Turn right to walk the third of a mile, on duckboards, crossing wet moorland, to see Britain's only rock-cut tomb. Return over the duckboarding to the road and turn right.

5 Head on, with a good view of Burra Sound and the island of Graemsay. Go on past a conifer plantation, where many trees have suffered wind-blow. The birch, rowan, aspen and whitebeam, planted close to the road, are low-growing and stunted. Then the pier and the blockship, *The Inverlaine*, come into view. At the T-junction, turn left onto the B-road and then, almost immediately, take the right fork where the road divides. Head on along the road to the next T-junction, where you turn right and then right again to return to the pier.

Aspen

If you have parked at the start of the Rackwick footpath, turn left at the first T-junction and then left again at the next.

Practicals

Type of walk: Rackwick footpath muddy in places.
Considerable quiet road walking through dramatic scenery.

Distance: 9 miles/14.5km
Time: 4 hours
Maps: OS Explorer 462 / Landranger 7

21

Old Man of Hoy

Old Man of Hoy

Take the roll-on roll-off ferry from Houton to Lyness pier (see details walk 20). Go ahead from the pier to turn north onto the B9047and drive for 8 miles along the narrow, scenic road. Then turn left and continue to the end of the road at Rackwick. Park in the public car park, where there are toilets, grid ref 202993.

The horizontally bedded and vertically jointed sandstones of north and west Hoy have resulted in a spectacular coastline of cliffs and stacks on the Atlantic seaboard. These culminate in **St John' Head** (1,136 ft /346m), one of the highest vertical cliffs in Britain, and the **Old Man of Hoy**, (450ft/137m) a sea stack and one of Orkney's most famous landmarks. It is the remains of a collapsed natural arch carved by the sea from a narrow promontory. At Brae Brough, the almost detached platform of rock at the highest point of St John's Head, the remains of a bank can be seen. While this could be defensive, it is more likely to be remnants

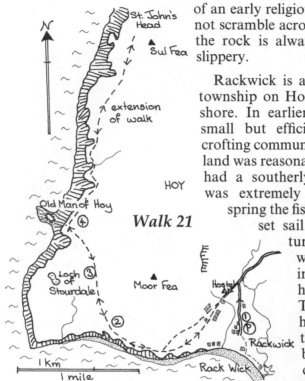

of an early religious hermitage. Do not scramble across to the Brough; the rock is always wet and very slippery.

Rackwick is a remote crofting township on Hoy's wild Atlantic shore. In earlier times it was a small but efficient fishing and crofting community. Although the land was reasonably sheltered and had a southerly aspect, fishing was extremely difficult. Every spring the fishing yawls would set sail. When they returned, the women waded waist-deep in the water to haul them ashore. Then they carried home the catch on their backs. The boats required a crew of four and fishing ceased in 1963 when not enough able-bodied men were left. The settlement became largely abandoned. Now many of the old houses are inhabited again or let as holiday accommodation.

1 Leave the parking area and bear right along the road. Then take the first left and then the second left to join a faint path that runs behind the youth hostel. Beyond, stride on as directed by way-marks. The path crosses a small burn. Look upstream to see a tiny waterfall, its crystal clear water hurrying through shadowing vegetation. From here you have a good view of the Rackwick Valley (walk 20). The way continues on as a narrow peaty path as you begin to ascend the slopes of Moor Fea. Pass through a kissing gate and stride on through the heather, bog asphodel, cotton grass and tormentil.

2 As the path curves round a sheltered hollow, there is more soil and bracken clothes the slopes, filling the air with its aroma.

Cotton grass

C.M.Isherwood

Enjoy the view of Rackwick Bay. Another signpost appears beside the path, reassuring you that you are on the right route. Stride on along the path. And then you have your first glimpse of the Old Man, the 450ft high sandstone stack. Where the path descends through a rocky area look for alpine bearberry, cowberry and crowberry growing beside the path.

3 Carry on past, on the left, the little loch of Stourdale. To the right large boulders litter the steep moorland slopes and here great skuas perch on heather–covered mounds. As the path leads towards the edge of the immensely steep cliffs the wind increases so take great care as you approach. Then you can see the magnificent pink-red stack in dramatic entirety. The first successful climb of the Old Man was in July 1966 by a team of three led by Chris Bonnington. It took them three days.

4 You may wish to extend your walk by continuing along the dramatic cliffs towards St John's Head, but progress with care. Return by the same route, with a pleasing vista ahead all the way.

Cowberry

Practicals

Type of walk: The peaty track is easy to walk. There is a steady climb at the start and a little scrambling is required. Boots advisable.

Distance: 5 miles/8km
Time: 2–3 hours
Maps: OS Explorer 462 / Landranger 7

N B You may wish to combine this walk with walk 20 to make a truly dramatic day.

22

Betty Corrigall's grave and Scad Head, Hoy

Park near the Water of Hoy in the layby for Betty Corrigall's grave, grid ref 281998. Access this from Lyness Pier heading north on the B9047 for 5 miles.

Betty Corrigal was a young girl who lived in Lyness during the 19th century. She was in love with a sailor, but he left Hoy on a ship and never returned. Upon realising she was pregnant she tried to drown herself. Neighbours pulled her out and then she hanged herself in the byre. At the time suicide was considered a sin so she could not be buried in consecrated ground. The lairds of Hoy and Melsetter refused her burial on their estates and as a result she was buried on the parish border. The grave was discovered in the early 1930s by peat cutters. In 1949 an American minister, the Rev. Kenwood Bryant,

Betty Corrigal's grave

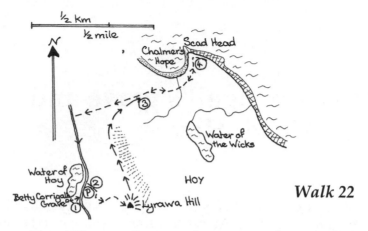

Walk 22

on a visit to Hoy, made a wooden cross and surrounded the grave with a picket fence. He asked Harry Berry, the Customs and Excise officer for Hoy, if he would make a gravestone and Mr Berry promised to do so when he had time. In 1976 he retired and found time to make the headstone. He wrote to Mr Bryant in the USA telling him he could now keep his promise. The minister replied that ' some people cannot keep a promise after 27 minutes let alone 27 years'. The land around the grave is a peat bog and a heavy stone would require a deep foundation. Betty's grave had been disturbed twice in previous years so Mr Berry decided to make the headstone of fibreglass to avoid disturbing the grave again. He and two friends then stood around the grave, one evening in 1976, and performed a short service.

1 Read the poem on the plaque in the layby:

> *So sweet*
> *So small*
> *Here lies Betty Corrigall*
> *Outwith the bounds of kin they buried her*
> *And not within*
> *The burn beside*
> *The brae above*
> *Keep her with more abundant love.*

Then walk down the peat track, from the layby, to the fenced, lonely grave. Look for red-throated divers on the Water of Hoy and then look downhill from the grave to a small plantation. Suddenly the grave doesn't seem quite so lonely. Return to the

90

road and walk north to take the red kissing gate on the right side of the road.

Red-throated diver

2 Beyond, follow the good track to the viewpoint on Lyrawa Hill, from where there is a wonderful panorama of Scapa Flow and the Mainland. Then walk left (north) to the derelict dugout of a 1939–45 anti-aircraft battery. Between the buildings, look for a small slab of shale with a white arrow on it. This directs you diagonally across the slope, keeping above the bracken. Carry on downhill, as directed by more arrowed slabs, until you reach a large metal wheel, once part of winding gear, and then go on a sharply sloping track dipping towards the headland.

3 Turn right and follow the route of what was once a railway track used for a coastal defence gun battery on the shore of the bay of Chalmers' Hope. Just before the derelict look-out buildings by the gun site, continue on a green track that leads to Scad Head and more look-outs. What a view the army had.

4 After a pause here return along the green path to rejoin the bed of the old railway track, which stretches uphill still, after 60 years, a great scar that can be seen from the ferry when you return. Continue past the winding wheel and carry on climbing to the road. Turn left to return to the layby.

Practicals

Type of walk: Short, tough little walk to Scad Head.

Distance: 2 miles/3.4km
Time: 1 hour
Maps: OS Explorer462 / Landranger 7

23

Westness Heritage walk, Rousay

The ferry for Rousay leaves Tingwall Pier on the Mainland. For information tel: 01856 751360. Booking essential. At the time of writing you need to back your vehicle on to the ferry. If you feel uncomfortable doing this, one of the crew will willingly do it for you.

Leave by the pier road and turn left at the T-junction. Drive for 4½ miles and park in the well-signposted layby, grid ref 375307.

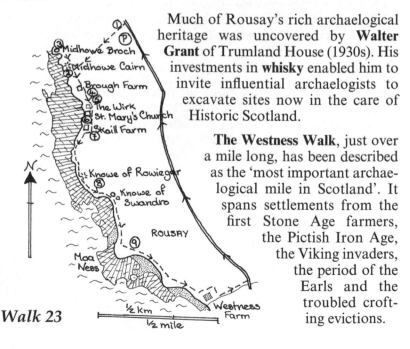

Much of Rousay's rich archaelogical heritage was uncovered by **Walter Grant** of Trumland House (1930s). His investments in **whisky** enabled him to invite influential archaelogists to excavate sites now in the care of Historic Scotland.

The Westness Walk, just over a mile long, has been described as the 'most important archaelogical mile in Scotland'. It spans settlements from the first Stone Age farmers, the Pictish Iron Age, the Viking invaders, the period of the Earls and the troubled crofting evictions.

Walk 23

Midhowe Cairn

1 Pass through the red painted kissing gate, following the signpost direction, in the layby, for Midhowe Cairn and Midhowe Broch. Drop down the steep slippery grassy slope to a white post and continue through another kissing gate. Walk on in the same direction to the next post. Beyond lies Eynhallow Sound with its fierce tide race.

2 Turn right along the shore to a large, sturdily constructed shed that shields Neolithic Midhowe Cairn, built around 3500 BC. Once inside, walk round the stalled and chambered cairn, the longest in Orkney and then climb to the slatted platforms, above, for an exciting overview. Look down to where the remains of 25 people were found lying facing inwards on the benches and chambers, and on the floor, in compartments formed by upright slabs. Animal bones were also found, showing the people were both hunters and gatherers. Such tombs as these were used for many generations. The roof might have been capped by turf.

3 Go on a few steps along the shore to see Midhowe Broch. This fine defensive structure, which could house a small community, stands on the rocky shore. Geos and creeks, on either side, effectively form a small and easily defensible promontory. On the landward side a strong wall stands between two ditches. Inside the broch there is a mass of slabs, cells and part-walls and you can see that there was once an upper floor. Look for the glassed-over hearth and for the stone-slabbed water trough with a neatly fitting lid, into which water seeped, providing for the broch. The water still seeps in today. The Iron Age people were dominated by a warrior aristocracy and the broch was probably a fortified residence of a petty chief and the community under his protection. Return along the shore, past the Midhowe Cairn to come to the ruin of Brough farm.

4 The farm was probably built in the 18th century. It has been empty since 1845, when the Traills, the landowners at the time, created Westness farm out of lands from which they had evicted the inhabitants during the clearances. Only the gable ends and a cupboard remain of Brough farm. Continue on, pausing occasionally to look down on to shore where you might spot seals hauled out on rocks. Carry on to The Wirk.

5 Little remains today of The Wirk which was once a 13th or 14th century ceremonial hall. The hall was at first-floor level, which is the level visible today and below was a basement of which you can just discern some parts. Leave the path, just before The Wirk

Common seal

by a kissing gate through the wall and then walk behind the ruin to pass through the wall by another kissing gate into the cemetery of St Mary's Church, the former parish church of Rousay.

6 It was abandoned in 1820, the standing ruin is probably of 16th or 17th century origin. The massive buttresses were added to the ruin in the late 19th century to keep the building from sliding down the slope. Look for the gravestone of James Sinclair, aged 75 years, who was shipwrecked, in October 1893, while crossing treacherous Eyenhallow Sound with the mailboat. Stroll on to the next kissing gate to walk through the ruined Skaill farm.

7 Like Brough farm, Skaill probably dates from the 18th century and has been empty since the clearances. Look for the round kiln in which barley was dried. By the ruins of two dwellings here, a plaque tells of the birth of innumerable children and how they all slept! Watch out for the arrow directing you towards the shore at the end of the ruins. The next gate takes you through the wall to the shore and is hidden from view until you have walked down beside the wall on the left. Do Not take the gap in the wall. Beyond continue in the same direction, now walking a rough path littered with stones thrown up by the sea. Carry on the clearly waymarked route along the flower-covered turf, from where you will be able to spot a variety of birds and probably more seals.

8 Go on past the Knowe of Rowieger, a chambered tomb and the Knowe of Swandro, a mound that contains the remains of a broch. There is little to see but imagination can do wonderful things. Near the latter stood two parallel long houses belonging to the Norse period of the 11th or 12th century. Carry on along the edge of the shore around Moa Ness promontory where, in 1963, a farmer digging a hole to bury a cow came across Pictish and Viking graves. Here an ornamental ringed pin, now known as the Westness Brooch, was found.

9 Further east, beyond the next marker post, stood a Viking noust. The Vikings could moor their boats here, even at low tide, and find shelter from the wind and strong tidal currents. On the inland side of the path stands a vast wet area, fringed with flags. Then carry on along a raised bank of stones, which makes for quite hard walking. Continue to the red kissing gate, on the left, in the wall, just before Westness farm. Beyond walk beside the

wall on your right. Pass through the next kissing gate to walk the farm access track. Turn left through the next gate to walk the road. At the virtually traffic-free road, turn left and walk the quiet way, for 1½ miles to the parking layby with, for all the way, glorious views of the Westness Walk and of the Sound beyond.

Dunlin

Practicals

Type of walk: Level walking but it can be rough under foot if the tide has thrown up debris on the more exposed parts of the path. This is a 'must' walk.

Distance: 3 miles/5km
Time: 2–3 hours
Maps: OS Explorer 464 / Landranger 6

24

Muckle Water and Peerie Water, Rousay

You may wish to combine this contrasting walk with the Westness Walk (23). As the track is on the land of **James Marwick, the farmer at Westness farm**, please ask for permission to use it, which he gives readily. Shut the gate encountered first, keep all dogs on leads and do not approach vulnerable nesting birds.

Park opposite the access to Westness farm, grid ref 384291.

1 Climb the track, opposite Westness farm, which climbs into the hills to the left of some cottages. Pass through the gate and continue with Ward Hill standing dark and sombre to your left. Between the track and the hill lies a steep ravine through which hurries a tiny burn, edged with flags in summer. As you ascend, the ravine becomes narrower and more steep-sided. The track

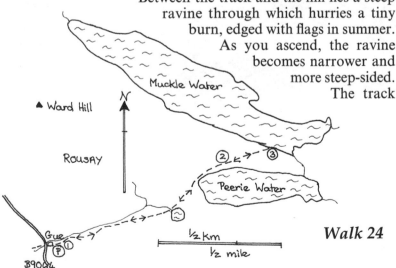

Walk 24

ascends steadily, with a wealth of flowers along its margins. Then you reach a small round dammed pool, with reeds fringing its edges.

2 Continue on to pass Peerie Water, a good trout loch, on whose banks grow two large clumps of salmon berry. Out in the middle of the still water you might spot a red-throated diver. Carry on along the track to reach the shore of the extensive Muckle Water, another trout loch. Here low growing willow thrives over the boulder-strewn shore.

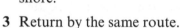

Iris

3 Return by the same route.

Muckle Water

Practicals

Type of walk: The clear track becomes a little rough in places as it takes you into the lonely hills.

Distance: 2 miles/3.4km
Time: 1 hour
Maps: OS Explorer 464 / Landranger 6

RSPB Trumland Reserve, short walk. Taversoe Tuick Cairn, Rousay

For this walk, and walk 25b, a car is not needed because the reserve lies close to the pier. If you wish to use your car, as you will need to in order to reach the other walks on Rousay, park at the pier, grid ref 436274, or in the layby, grid ref 429275, signed for Taversoe Tuick. To reach the island see details for walk 23.

Trumland House is a Jacobean style mansion, built for General Sir Frederick Traill Burroughs. His uncle, George William Traill, evicted 210 people during the Clearances in the mid-19th century,

Trumland House

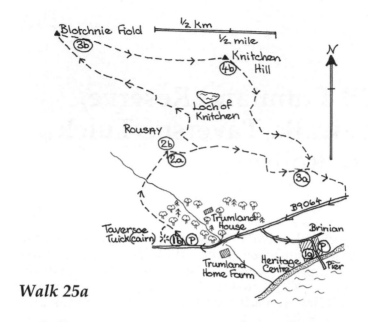

Walk 25a

the only people in Orkney to suffer such a fate. He removed the people as part of his modernisation of his Westness estate.

To gain access to **Taversoe Tuick Cairn**, walk past it to go through a gate at the top of the enclosure. Under the cairn's turf roof a concrete dome has a glass window, which allows plenty of light for viewing the well preserved site. The cairn is two-storeyed and a mesh gate gives access to the top level. The upper chamber is divided into two and it has a recess in one of its walls. A metal ladder enables you to view the lower chamber, which was originally entered by a long passage at a lower level. It is divided into four compartments. Here skeletal remains, including a crouched skeleton, were discovered, resting on shelves. Lower still is a small chamber protected by a heavy trapdoor.

1 Walk up the road from the ferry terminal and at the T-junction, turn left. Continue past Trumland House on the right. Opposite the stately house is Trumland home farm. Continue along the road to pass the woodland of the big house, then climb, right, to a signposted kissing gate. Pass through to the start the trail and for the entrance to Taversoe Tuick Cairn, which is well worth a visit. Return from the cairn and join the trail track and continue

uphill to another kissing gate beside a white-topped post. This post is the first of many that directs you through the reserve. Beyond the gate lies an old quarry. Head on to cross a narrow ford and carry on over a dampish area to an old wall and a ditch.

2 Beyond, follow the posts to pass a large bank of fuchsia. Go on through heather and enjoy the retrospective extensive views. At the marker post for the 'long trail' (25b), turn right. Walk the peaty track, following the posts, from where you can see the islands of Wyre and of Egilsay. Look for Wideford Hill and Kirkwall on the Mainland. Follow the track as it swings right and then left. Below you can see Rousay pier and Wyre pier. At the telegraph pole this short walk is joined by the path that is part of the RSPB's longer trail (25b).

3 The path descends steadily through heather and bushes of gorse and fuchsia. Continue to a white marker post where the arable land begins. Cross a plank footbridge, turn left, climb a stile and walk along the edge of a pasture. Climb the next stile to the narrow road and turn right. Turn left at the sign-post for the pier. Leave time to visit the Trumland Visitors Centre to view the exhibition on all aspects of Rousay. There is a waiting room, toilets and a picnic area here.

Fuschia

Practicals

Type of walk: Parts are rough and wet. Views excellent.

Distance: 2 miles/3.4km
Time: 1 hour
Maps: OS Explorer 464 / Landranger 6

25b

RSPB Trumland Reserve, longer walk

Park either at the pier, or, drive to the T-junction and turn left. Continue on to the parking layby, on the right, just beyond the woodland of Trumland House, signed for Taversoe Tuick cairn, grid ref 429275.

Corncrake

The **RSPB** has over 8000 hectares of reserves in Orkney and is involved in projects to care for Orkney's **hen harrier** and **corncrake** populations. On the Trumland Reserve look for hen harriers, short-eared owls, merlins, golden plovers, curlews, ravens, great northern divers, red throated divers and gulls.

1 From the layby, walk up the slope to go through a kissing gate. Go ahead following the white-topped posts. Continue past an old quarry and cross a small burn. At the wall, climb the stile and pass onto the open moorland.

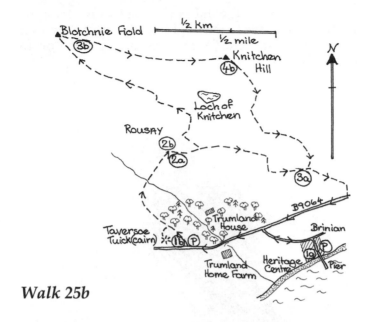

Walk 25b

2   Follow the posts past fuchsia bushes. Continue climbing and then turn left onto a narrower path banked with heather and crowberry. The path climbs and curves right. Follow an arrow directing you left to a post marked '2'. (The right turn is the route for the shorter walk 25a.) Look back to see Loch of Knitchen. Continue on along an old peat track, heading for Blotchnie Fiold, the highest point up to your left. From this high point (250m) the views are superb and take in Westray, Eday, Sanday and North Ronaldsay. This is a great place for a picnic and to watch, perhaps, skylarks, golden plover, and curlews.

3   Walk east along the ridge, following the posts to the cairn and the trig point on Knitchen Hill (227m). The views are spectacular from here. See if you can spot the lighthouse on North Ronaldsay.

4   From the cairn, follow the ever-helpful posts, descending steadily over acres of heather in the direction of the road, which you can see below. As you go you might spot a hen harrier quartering the ground. Head on down to where the shorter walk (25a) joins from the right. Press on down past gorse and fuchsia to a marker post at the wall between the moorland and the arable land. Cross

a plank footbridge, turn left, climb a stile and walk along the edge of a pasture to the stile to the road and turn right. Carry on along the road and turn, left, for the pier or, continue on to return to the parking layby.

Merlin

Practicals

Type of walk: This is a tougher walk, often pathless and wet underfoot. Parts are over heather and through peaty areas. It is challenging but the rewards are the spectacular views from the tops and the chance of spotting some exciting birds.

Distance: 4 miles/6.5km
Time: 3 hours
Maps: OS Explorer 464 / Landranger 6

26

Faraclett Head, Rousay

Park in the well signed parking area, just along the access track to Faraclett Head farm, grid ref 447324. To reach this, leave the pier, drive up the hill to the T-junction, where you turn right. Drive on for about two miles. To reach Rousay see details for walk 23.

Faraclett Head

Faraclett Head has a terraced appearance that was brought about by glaciation. The part of the route which follows these terraces is waymarked. The coastal cliffs on the north-west side of the headland are marked on early maps as 'overhanging' therefore the sloping grassy sward above, which can be slippery, should be treated with respect. Keep to the waymarked route, well away from the edge. The Head is a mixture of maritime heath and moorland and it supports a rich variety of plants. Some common species grow only an inch above ground level and thereby manage to survive the challenging conditions

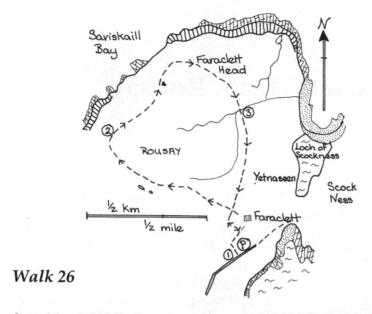

Walk 26

found here. While desolate in winter, the heath comes to life in the summer with colonies of sea birds and a profusion of small flowering plants such as grass of Parnassus and *Primula scotica*. Part of Faraclett Head is a SSSI and management is by limited sheep grazing to maintain the heath in prime condition.

1 Walk up the farm track to climb the waymarked stile. Go on uphill to climb the next stile. Then head on up, slightly right, to a tall waymarked post, the first of many. Continue, right, across the pasture to join the farm track, ignoring the waymarked gate ahead (your return route). Turn left up the muddy track to a waymarked gate – if locked use the stone stile to the left. Bear left and climb the muddy way (after rain) to a waymark ahead, placed on a plinth of stones. From now on the mud is left behind and the slightly indistinct path, a joy to walk, passes through low growing heather and sphagnum, with small rocks breaking through the surface. The way climbs steadily to a tall waymark on a hillock in the distance. To your left is a shallow valley with small pools, like a string of beads.

2 And then as you wind right the lovely curve of Saviskaill Bay comes into view, with very steep grassy slopes descending almost

to the water's edge. From here you can begin to see Orkney's north isles coming into view. At the right time of the year you might see, about the slopes, curlews, arctic skuas, great skuas, arctic terns, oyster catchers, and meadow pipits. Carry on to the next waymark as it directs you well up, away from the cliff edge. Bear steadily right until you can see the Holm of Scockness and Egilsay and continue to Faraclett Head. Carry on slightly downhill.

3 Then the waymarks lead you steadily right along one of the terraces, heading towards a ladderstile over a wall. Bear a little right to walk beside the wall on your right. Climb another ladderstile and carry on to the next waymark. On the next post is written Yetnaseen, the name given to a massive standing stone away to your left, which you might like to visit. It is said that it walks to the nearest loch for a drink each New Year! Continue on to the next waymark and walk ahead across the next pasture. Cross the farm track, keep ahead to the waymark standing in the middle of the pasture and then descend, left, to climb the ladderstiles taken at the outset of the walk and continue along the track to the parking area.

Grass of Parnassus

Practicals

Type of walk: An airy ramble high above hidden cliffs. Wonderful views, pleasing vegetation and lots of bird life.

Distance: 2½ miles/4km
Time: 2 hours
Maps: OS Explorer 464 / Landranger 6

27

Eday Heritage walk

*Stone of
Setter*

Park close to Eday Community Co-op Shop, grid ref 569367. To access this, leave the ferry, bear right along the B9063 and follow it where it bears right again at Roadside. Continue on for about 4 miles to go past London airport! In the summer the ferry leaves from Kirkwall throughout the week. Book the day before.

The **Stone of Setter** is a colossal monolith standing, nearly 15ft high, in a meadow of flowering grasses, near Mill Loch. It is festooned with lichen and sometimes there is a rough twiggy nest in a groove near the top. Do not approach the loch but view it from the excellent hide, from where you might spot several pairs of red-throated divers.

C.M. Isherwood

Walk 27

West Toe
East Toe
Red Head
Noup Hill
③
EDAY
Calf Sound
Bay of Carrick
Vinquoy Hill
④
Carrick House
Vinquoy Hill Cairn
②
Chambered Cairns
Old School
Fold of Setter
N
Stone of Setter
Hide
Mill Loch
①
P
½ Km
½ mile

Vinquoy Hill chambered cairn is a small tomb, which dates from before 2,000BC. The tomb was a burial chamber for the local community and the central chamber has four cells opening from it. It is approached by crawling, or walking crouched, along a narrow passage. The red sandstone that forms the walls was probably obtained from the small quarries around the site. It is beehive-shaped and was restored in 1985 and a sympathetic small dome added to allow in daylight. The exquisite tomb is of the Maeshowe type and even the claustrophobic cannot fail to be amazed by the wonderful construction.

Carrick House, a 17th century laird's dwelling, was built, in 1633, by the younger brother of Earl Patrick Stewart, who commissioned the building of the Earl's Palace in Kirkwall. Here in 1725 John Gow, the pirate, was taken prisoner after grounding on the Calf of Eday. Notice the four cannon pointing out to sea.

1 Walk up the narrow road opposite the shop, signposted for the heritage walk. Beyond Mill Loch, heather covers the

109

slopes of Resting Hill. Pause in the hide and then go on up the road to take a signposted path, right, to the Stone of Setter. Stride on beyond the waymarked kissing gate to continue over duckboards in the direction of what looks like a barn but once was a school. Close by, try to discern a large circular enclosure, almost 300ft in diameter. This is the Fold of Setter and maybe all that is left of a prehistoric enclosure for livestock. Pass over more duckboards. To the right of the next waymarker post are the remains of a large chambered tomb, now roofless. Follow the waymarked posts over rough grass to see Huntersquoy tomb, which once had two storeys, similar to Taversoe Tuick on Rousay, walk 25a.

2 Bear left to climb Vinquoy Hill. By the signpost, look right to see a neolithic turf wall. Continue climbing to the signpost on top of the ridge. It stands beside the Vinquoy chambered tomb, over 4,000 years old. Stroll on along the ridge. Ahead you can see the Calf of Eday in its entirety. Across to the left lies Faray and the Holm of Faray. The path continues through hummocks of heather and crowberry, littered with pieces of warm red sandstone. From the summit cairn, on a clear day, you can see the northern isles, the Mainland of Orkney and Fair Isle of Shetland. Stride to the wall ahead and turn right as directed by the signpost, to descend to Vinquoy Hill plantation. The wood is composed of stunted and twisted European larch and lodgepole pine. Alders grow. A dense growth of gorse surrounds the plantation. Pass through a kissing gate to continue along the side of the hill, overlooking Calf Sound, with its small brilliant white lighthouse. Descend to a valley where there are two signposts. This walk follows the path for Noup Hill.

3 Climb straight up Noup Hill and continue over a dense mat of heather. Now you are level with the northern tip of the Calf of Eday, with its several dramatic natural arches. Beyond you can see Sanday. Where the track ends, head left for the fence

Gorse

110

above the cliffs, where the vegetation changes to ankle-twisting tussocks of grass. Peat cutting took place here on an industrial scale in the 19th century. Wind round West Toe, to your left, to come to the trig point (230ft/70m) and pause here to enjoy the views. Return alongside the fence, keeping the sturdy waymarked fence, and then a wall, to your right, with occasional glimpses of the sea far below. Follow the indistinct way, along the west side of Noup Hill, taking care as you go as the heather conceals many ankle traps. Drop down the slope to the two signposts seen earlier. Follow the one for Carrick House. Keep to the track that heads towards the gracious house.

4 More signposts direct you on, keeping well above the shore, to a kissing gate close to the house. As this is a private house no approach should be made along the shore. Keep to the outside wall of the house and pass through a gate to the narrow road, where you turn right. At the home farm turn left and continue on to the T-junction, where you turn right to return to where you have parked.

Great Northern Diver in winter

Practicals

Type of walk: This route, in the north of the island, encompasses pre-history, archaeology, natural history, industrial archaeology and much more.

Distance: 5 miles/8km
Time: 3–4 hours
Maps: OS Explorer 464 / Landranger 5

28

Warness Walk, Eday

Park in the car park on the Greentoft road, adjacent to the beach, grid ref 558289. To reach this, leave the pier at Eday by the B960 and drive, or walk, the three-quarters of a mile to where it turns sharp right at Roadside. Here turn left and drive (or walk) for just under a mile to park. See walk 27 for access to the island.

Eday is situated among the North Isles of Orkney and lies 14 miles north-east of Kirkwall. It offers heather-clad hilly moorland from where there are panoramic views over sea and islands, sheer cliffs, sweeping beaches and sand dunes. Most of the crofts and farms are located on the fertile coastal strip. It is known as the isthmus isle, eight miles long and pinched in at the waist between the Bay of Doomy and the Bay of London.

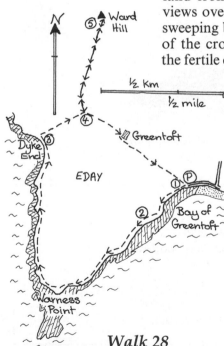

Walk 28

This walk is well waymarked and is within easy reach of the ferry pier. It provides a good walk for those who perhaps have come for the day and have not brought their car. To the east of the start of the walk and east of the croft of Maltburn, is a large low mound called Stackelbrae or the Hammer. It is the site of the **Castle of Stackelbrae,**

112

Razorbills

a small Norse castle, dating from the between the 11th and 13th centuries. Today, all that can be seen on the surface is the mound, but in the eroding shoreline stonework is visible. It is believed that Pirate Gow's men (see walk 27) were taken here after their capture at Carrick to await transportation to London. At that time (1725) the lower parts of the castle, the dungeon, were still intact.

Each island has a **Ward Hill** or Beacon Hill. Here a beacon was lit to warn of the approach of enemies when the Vikings ruled in Orkney.

1 From the car park walk, west, along the coast outside the farm fence. Continue along the shore to the point where a small burn flows into the sea. Here look for scattered stones, all that remains of an early chapel, Hannah's Kirk. The burn is the overflow from Lady Well, now covered by a building. It is the biggest spring on Eday and produces pure water.

2 Carry on along the coast to Warness Point. From here, look out to sea to Muckle Green Holm and Little Green Holm, now nature reserves. They have been uninhabited since the Middle Ages. Between the Holms and the Point runs a strong tide. From the Point enjoy the superb view of Hoy, Shapinsay, Rousay, Gairsay, Egilsay and Stronsay. Then climb the signed stile and continue on along the outside of the cliff fence, in a north-easterly direction. Take care as you go as the cliff edge crumbles easily. Here you might spot puffins and razorbills.

3 Where the route turns inland at Dyke End, *Spring squills* the soil changes. Look for sea pinks, squill and wild thyme. Eventually you reach a stile and from here waymarks direct you, south-east, beside a wall to an old sheepfold and shepherd's house used until recently for lambing and dipping. (If you wish to climb Ward Hill see point 4, below.) The track then goes on to Greentoft. The old house, in the shape of a Norse longhouse, dates from the 16th century. Today it is used as a byre. The new house dates from 1895. Then follow the waymarks to return to Greentoft Bay and the parking area.

4 To extend this walk, turn left at the sheepfold and ascend, diagonally, the heather and grass-clad Ward Hill, 334ft/101m, the highest point on Eday. From the summit enjoy the spectacular views over Eday and the other North Isles.

5 Return down the hill and follow the signs to Greentoft and then on to the car park.

Practicals

Type of walk: Short, easy and flat unless you ascend Ward Hill from where you will enjoy panoramic views.

Distance: 2¼ miles/3.8km. Add on a mile for Ward Hill.
Time: 1 or 2 hours
Maps: OS Explorer 465 / Landranger 5

29

Noup Head, Westray

Park at the end of the track by the lighthouse, grid ref 402498. The roll-on roll-off ferry from Kirkwall berths at Rapness. From here drive along the B9066 to Pierowall and leave the large village by a minor road, west, in

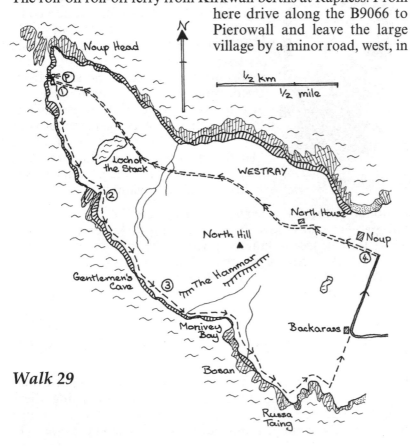

Walk 29

the direction of Noltland Castle. Beyond, drive on to pass Noup farm and then take the continuing way to the lighthouse at the north end of the RSPB reserve.

The very white **Noup Head lighthouse** was completed in 1898 by David A Stevenson, the last of the 'Lighthouse Stevensons' and first cousin of Robert Louis. The tower is 24m high and the light flashes every 30 seconds. It was automated in 1964 and in 2001 solar power replaced gas, with the use of 36 solar panels.

Guillemots

1 Walk south along the magnificent old red sandstone cliffs, with the sea to your right. The horizontal rock structure composed of innumerable 'plates' of rock, provides unlimited sites for the thousands of nesting guillemots, kittiwakes, some razorbills and fulmars. The smell from the droppings of these birds in the breeding season can be overpowering. The nearby waters provide a large amount of food for this huge number of birds. Head on along the spectacular cliffs over the short turf, which supports sea thrift, squill and plantain.

2 Continue on to pass two extremely deep geos. Then you can see a tall high cave far below. Next comes John Harcus's windows, where the cliff face, regularly fluted by the action the sea, really does look like a row of windows. Press on until just before you descend the Hammar. The Gentlemen's Cave lies in the sea cliffs far below. It can be reached from the cliff top, but you are advised not to attempt a descent without a local guide. Several Orkney lairds 'retired' to this cave after supporting the 1745 Jacobite Rebellion until their unfortunate allegiance was forgotten.

3 Carry on the path along the edge of the cliffs to wind round Monivey bay. Continue above the Bosan and Russa Taing where rocky skerries jut out into the white topped water. Look out to sea where you might spot whales, dolphins and porpoises. On calm days they are occasionally seen off the coast. Start to curve round north-east with views of natural arches below and then head inland on a track to Backarass. Beyond, continue on the narrow road to Noup.

4 Turn left and return along the road, driven earlier. Go on past Loch of the Stack where you might see kittiwakes idling the afternoon away on the still water. Head on along the road to rejoin your car.

John Harcus's Windows

Practicals

Type of walk: Fine cliff walk with spectacular views, vast numbers of sea birds and an abundance of flowers. Generally easy walking along the path but beware dangerous cliffs. The return is made along the quiet narrow road to the lighthouse.

Distance: 4½ miles/7.4km
Time: 3–4 hours
Maps: OS Explorer 464 / Landranger 5

30

Westray Coast (linear walk)

Park at East Kirbest on the west Westray coast, grid ref 428437. To reach this, drive north from Rapness on the B9066 for 5 miles. Turn left on a B-road and go on to join the B9067, where you turn left again. Follow this to Gary, where you turn right to East Kirbest. To reach the island see details walk 29.

Westray is Orkney's most north-westerly island. It has an 80km coastline with superb cliff scenery and glorious sandy bays. The rocks of the island are made up of thick layers of flagstones, which have been used for centuries for roofs, buildings and paving stones.

1 The start of the walk is clearly signposted. The path takes you through West Kirbest and then on below Skea Hill, with the Atlantic to your left. The way is stiled and these delineate your route. Carry on below Fitty Hill, where the cliffs are very high and great care should be taken. On this dramatic cliff top you might spot the rare Scottish primrose.

Scottish primrose

2 As you continue the way becomes more and more breathtaking with great views of caves, natural arches, headlands and of thundering Atlantic rollers but great care should be taken on the cliff edge.

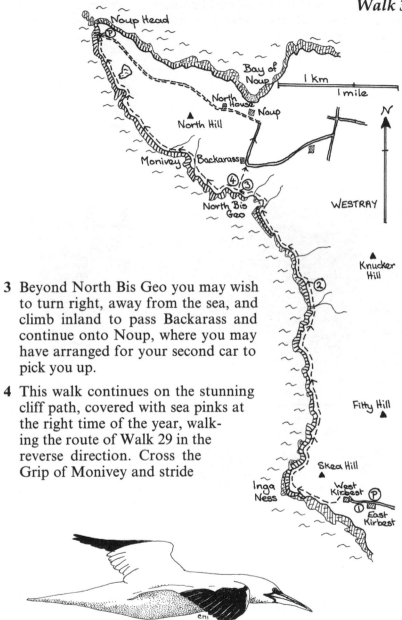

3 Beyond North Bis Geo you may wish to turn right, away from the sea, and climb inland to pass Backarass and continue onto Noup, where you may have arranged for your second car to pick you up.

4 This walk continues on the stunning cliff path, covered with sea pinks at the right time of the year, walking the route of Walk 29 in the reverse direction. Cross the Grip of Monivey and stride

Gannet

119

on below North Hill (240ft/76m) and on until you reach Noup Head and the lighthouse, where you may have arranged to pick up your second car.

Noup Head

Practicals

Type of walk: A stunning cliff path linear walk, one of the best in Orkney. Two cars, one at East Kirbest and the other at the lighthouse, would make this an easier walk or you may prefer to turn back when you feel you have gone far enough. Or you could arrange for a taxi from Pierowall to return you to your car. Some people will want to return by the same path (11 miles). See walk 29 for a circular walk from the lighthouse. Walking boots and waterproofs essential.

Distance: 5½ miles/8.8km, one way
Time: 3–4 hours walking time, one way
Maps: OS Explorer 464 / Landranger 5

Noltland Castle, Westray

Park close to Noltland Castle, which lies on a minor road west of Pierowall, grid ref 429489. To reach Westray see details walk 29.

Picturesque **Noltland Castle** was a fortified residence, built in the 16th century for Gilbert Balfour, who served Mary, Queen of Scots, and aided in the plot to murder her second husband, Lord Darnley. It was constructed of huge blocks of stone, and has shot holes and windows. The most spectacular feature is the spiral staircase, with a smaller one higher up in the living area of the castle. Legend has it that the castle is linked with the Gentlemen's Cave mentioned in Walk 29. It is a wonderful fortress to explore and must seem magical to all children. It is dramatic from the outside, with its many gun loops, but inside is even more so.

Over the wire fencing, among the dunes, is the site of an **archaeological dig**. Here in the late 1970s an extensive area of prehistoric settlement was excavated. The houses and middens were contemporary with Skara Brae (3000BC). The excavations have been covered over.

Noltland Castle

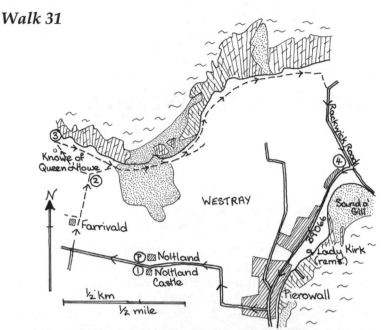

The **Vikings** appreciated Pierowall's natural harbour and named it Hofn, which means harbour. At that time it was the only Norse village in Orkney. On The Links was found a large Viking cemetery.

1 Leave the castle by the gate and turn left, west, to walk the narrow road until it turns sharp left. Here turn right and walk the reinforced cart track to its end. Pass through a gate on the right onto the links of Noltland. Look for many lichen-covered low walls of stone, known as dykes. These were for drying seaweed, tangle. The tangle was collected in the autumn after gales had broken off the great strands and they had come ashore.

Kelp

2 Carry on left, west, over the shallow turf, following the fence towards a sandy bay, where skerries turn the breakers white. Go on to pass the Knowe of Queen o' Howe, a green mound on the shore, which contains the foundations of an Iron Age broch. Stroll on over the flower covered turf (machair), passing through two Orkney gates, and on to a drystone wall. This is the end of land belonging to the farmer who lives opposite the castle and who is the keyholder for the castle.

3 Return along the shore past shallow depressions where the sea-weed was burnt to produce kelp, once used in glass and soap making and for obtaining iodine. Head on along the lovely sandy beach. Over the wire fencing on the right, among the dunes, is the archaeological dig site. Beyond the dig lies the golf course. Carry on to step across a small burn and stroll on along the shore until you reach the Rackwick road. Here bear right and join the B9066.

4 Turn right to go past the Sand o' Gill and on into the small bustling village of Pierowall. Here visit Lady Kirk, an attractive ruin dating back to the 13th century. It was still in use in the late 19th century when the village was a busy fishing port. At the school turn right, away from the shore, and follow the road as it bears right and then left to return to the parking area at Noltland Castle.

Lapwing

Practicals

Type of walk: An easy circular walk from a castle, along a glorious stretch of shoreline to explore a broch, tangle dykes, and onto an attractive village with a medieval church. Some quiet road walking.

Distance:	4½ miles/7.4km
Time:	2–3 hours
Maps:	OS Explorer 464 / Landranger 5

32

Tuquoy, Westside Cross Kirk and Mae Sand, Westray

Leave your vehicle in the parking area on the shore of the Bay of Tuquoy, grid ref 455437. To reach this leave Pierowall, south, by the B9067. Where the road turns sharp right for East Kirbest (walk 30), turn left and follow the narrow road along the south side of the bay. To reach Westray see details walk 29.

Cross Kirk is believed to have been built by the Viking Haflidi of Tuquoy. It was dedicated to the Holy Cross. The square-ended chancel, which was vaulted, and the east end of the nave, were built in the 12th century. The west end of the nave was a later addition. The original entrance and the only surviving window are still preserved in the south wall of the nave.

Cross Kirk

Walk 33

Papay. It has around 70 inhabitants. It is renowed for its bird life, its archaeology, its wonderful beaches and most recently its attempt to sustain a genuine and distinctive small, integrated community.

1 Set off north west from the pier to wind west round Bothican, a fine sandy bay close to the New Pier (the latter has a waiting room and toilet). Continue round the stiled Bay of Moclett and then carry on north along the coast to reach the Minister's Flag. At one time the Westray minister had to land here and walk below the high tide line to his kirk, St Bonniface, because he had quarrelled with the laird, who would not let him walk on his land.

2 Carry on along the path to reach the Knap of Howar, a neolithic farmhouse cared for by Historic Scotland, who provide an information panel. It tells that the settlement was established about 3500BC. It lies well back from the seashore in a grassy area separated by dunes from a broad sandy bay. Over the years the ruins were buried in sand, then revealed again. It is the oldest known building in Orkney and in Northern Europe.

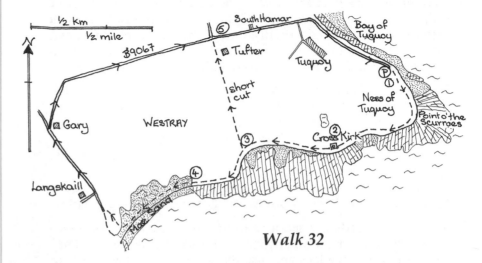

Walk 32

1 Stroll on to pass through the red kissing gate to walk the fenced track that keeps close to the lovely shore. Continue round the Point o' the Scurroes to pass through the next kissing gate. Beyond, great plates of red sandstone project out into the water. Across Westray Firth you can see the high hills of Rousay.

2 Climb the ladderstile into the graveyard of Cross Kirk. After you have visited the ruin, look at the dates on some of the headstones. A moving script gives the following details of deaths in one family:

James died aged two
William twenty-six
Isabella fourteen
Mary Ann twenty-five
Jessie fourteen
George killed in the First World War twenty-seven
Thomas also died in the Great War
Their father lived until he was seventy-four.

Leave the church by the gate and walk a few yards to the shore. Here in the low cliffs can be seen the edge of a large Norse settlement. The sea is gradually eroding the cliffs but you can see some of the midden and stones of a dwelling. This area was extensively excavated thirty years ago.

3 Pass through the next gate and, if you wish to make this a shorter walk, turn right and carry on inland to the crossroads, where you turn right and then right again along the bay to the parking area. This walk continues on past some old stone boat nousts, which were used to shelter fishing boats from the winter storms.

4 Continue on along the wild Mae Sand, where dunes stretch inland. This is a beautiful beach where, if the weather is right, you will want to idle. Head over the sand until you can turn inland and walk a track to Langskaill farm. Here was discovered a Viking longhouse with an Iron Age earth house below it. Stride on along the road to Gary to join the B9067 and bear right. At the crossroads, stroll on ahead to pass an old croft, South Hamar, a 'but and ben'. Look for its kiln used for drying barley.

5 Stroll on towards the sea and follow the way as it continues above the shore. Here you might see turnstones as you go. They have bright orange legs and use their pick-axe bill as levers to throw over large stones to get at small crabs and sand hoppers. Continue along the flower-bordered way to rejoin your car.

Turnstone

Practicals

Type of walk: A delightful coastal walk to a fine ruin and a grand sandy beach. Some quiet road walking.

Distance: 4 miles/6.5km
Time: 2–3 hours
Maps: OS Explorer 464 / Landranger 5

33

Papa Westray

There is now a stiled path all round the coast of Papa Westray so park where you wish to start your walk. This walk starts from the pier, grid ref 495494. Westray and Papa Westray can be reached independently by ro-ro ferry or by aeroplane. Both islands are also linked in just thirty minutes by passenger ferry, or in two minutes by the world's shortest scheduled commercial flight. It is also possible to make one part of the visit by sea and return by air, or vice-versa.

The brochures describe **Papa Westray** as Westray's 'little sister'. It is about six square miles in extent. The locals call it

Knap of Howar

3 Stroll on along the shore over great flags of sandstone. Beware in summer of young fulmars, plump and downy, sitting on their ledge waiting to be fed. When disturbed they can, with some accuracy, eject a stream of a strong-smelling oily substance. Soon you reach St Bonniface Kirk. Enter the churchyard through a gate to where fuchsia grows close beside the orange-lichened walls. To the east side a wooden cover shields a Norse hog-backed gravestone. Lift the cover. The gravestone is shaped like a longhouse and in the sunlight you can just make out patterning on what would have been the roof. Go into the church, which has been carefully restored, and enjoy its immense peace after the wind outside. Its walls date from the 12th century. The church stands on an area known as 'Monker Hoose', a huge Bronze-Age settlement of the medieval period. Here the midden and stone-work of the settlement are being gradually eroded by the sea.

4 Follow the stiled path to reach North Hill nature reserve. This wild and windswept reserve is managed by the people of Papay by controlled grazing in conjunction with the RSPB. Please remember visitors must NOT walk through the arctic tern colony. An information board requests that, if you are walking during the May, June or July breeding season you should remain on the path round the edge of the cliffs. Stroll north over the maritime sedge heath. Look for sea thrift, thyme, crowberry, bearberry, scabious, field gentians and large numbers of grass of Parnassus. Continue past shallow depressions where seaweed was burnt to produce kelp. Now the hollows are colonised by

Arctic terns

low-growing willow, making the most of the shelter. To the west the huge Atlantic rollers pound the rugged sandstone shore.

5 Pass round Mull Head where the cliffs are very steep and densely populated by birds. At this very tip of Papay is the Bore, a tidal race where the Atlantic crashes into the North Sea. Head on round, now walking south. Stroll over the top of Fowl Craig, a nesting site for large numbers of seabirds. Close views of the birds can be enjoyed from a wide platform of rock close by. The last great auk was shot here in 1813. It is now on display in the Natural History Museum in London. On reaching a stone wall, walk to the right and begin looking for the Scottish primrose. This rare diminutive plant is thought to have survived the Ice Age. On each small plant, look for several tiny pinkish purple flowers, each with a yellow centre or 'eye'.

6 Head on, south of Fowl Craig, where you pass small enclosures, known as 'crues', used for growing vegetables or penning geese. Then you pass North Wick and South Wick, two lovely bays of sparkling white sand and a good place to spot both common and grey seals, basking on the tidal reefs. Across the bay you can see the Holm of Papa and its ancient cairns (burial chambers). To visit the Holm ask at the Co-op about a boat which allows one hour on the island.

7 Walk on to see the Old Pier where the steamer from Kirkwall called once a week before the New Pier was built in 1970. It is now used by local lobster boats and for access to the Holm of Papay. From here you may wish to head inland if you would like to visit the co-operative shop, the post office, craft shop, the Papay Museum at Holland farm, Beltane guest house/ hostel complex (in converted farmworkers cottages), more B&Bs, school, or the toilets.

8 Then continue on round the coastal path. At Nouster look for boat nousts once used for giving shelter to boats. These can be found all round the shores of Papay indicating the presence of hundreds of boats in earlier years. Stroll on the lovely way to come to an isolated headland and an old water mill, used about 100 years ago for milling oats. You can still see two millstones and the remains of what would have been an undershot wheel made necessary by the low level of the Loch of St Tredwell, which lies to the west of the mill.

9 Further on along the way you might spot, on a small peninsula, jutting into the loch, traces of an Iron Age fortification and the walls of a medieval chapel and beehive cells, a place of pilgrimage until the 18th century. Then wander on until you reach the New Pier once more.

Field Gentian

Practicals

Type of walk: You can now walk around the whole island along the coast. It has stiles all the way round.

Distance:	11 miles /17km. If you wish to break up your walk you can stroll in from the west coast (Knap of Howar) or the east coast (the old pier) to pick up a taxi (tel 644202) to return you to the pier. You might also be offered a lift. No one on the island will go past you without waving or stopping for a chat.
Time:	6–7 hours
Maps:	OS Explorer 464 / Landranger 5

34

North Ronaldsay

m.v. Earl Thorfinn and m.v. Earl Sigurd carry both passengers and vehicles from Kirkwall to North Ronaldsay, weather conditions permitting. For details tel 01856 872044. At the time of writing Loganair offer a special overnight stay fare of £12. For details tel 01856 872494. It may be possible to make one part of your visit by sea and return by air, or vice versa.

North Ronaldsay, with a population of about 60, is the most remote of the northern isles. Its narrow roads, almost traffic-free, are a joy to walk. It lies further north than the southern tip of Norway but its climate is far less severe, due to the influence of the Gulf Stream. Because of its remoteness life on the island is in many ways different from the other islands.

A 13–mile stone dyke surrounds the island and outside this, on a narrow strip of beach and foreshore, live the island's **seaweed-eating sheep**. They are brought inside the wall at lambing time. At clipping and dipping time the sheep are herded off the beach into stone-built 'punds' by the collective efforts of the island's sheep farmers. Some of their iodine-rich meat is sold to up-market restaurants in London, but that happens mainly in winter when the sheep are in prime condition

North Ronaldsay sheep

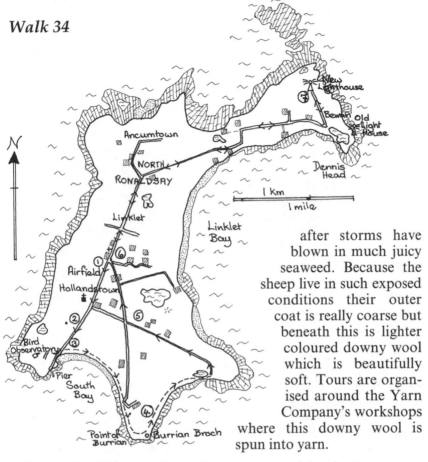

N

Ancumtown

NORTH
RONALDSAY

Linklet

Linklet
Bay

Airfield
Hollandstown

Bird
Observatory
Pier
South
Bay

Point of
Burrian

Burrian Broch

New
Lighthouse

Bewan Old
Light
House

Dennis
Head

1 Km

1 mile

after storms have blown in much juicy seaweed. Because the sheep live in such exposed conditions their outer coat is really coarse but beneath this is lighter coloured downy wool which is beautifully soft. Tours are organised around the Yarn Company's workshops where this downy wool is spun into yarn.

1 From the airfield walk to the war memorial, where you turn right. Stride along the road to pass, on your left, the stately Holland House, owned by a descendant of the family who bought North Ronaldsay in 1727. Standing in front of the house are three cannon salvaged from a ship, *Crown Prince*, which was wrecked off the island in 1744. On the right is an attractive church built in the early 1800s. Beyond, in a field is a standing stone over 13 ft/5m high. Look for the hole, through its upper part, which is believed to have been used as a calendar in conjunction with a stone. Or it might have been an out marker for the stone circle, which stood on Tor Ness.

2 Stride on in the direction of the pier and take the lane on the right, just before the cattle grid, to walk to North Ronaldsay's bird observatory. This is where those walkers arriving by the ferry would join the walk and turn left to the bird observatory. Here visitors are made welcome. If the mist descends and the plane cannot get through you might like to take advantage of the reasonably priced accommodation, in the low energy building, and perhaps help with the recording of observations.

3 Return to the cattle grid, which you do not cross, but instead pass through a gate opposite onto the silvery sands of Nouster Bay. Walk east, taking care in June and July not to disturb the fulmars nesting against the wall (sheep dyke) that stands between the pasture and the shore. Look for the hardy sheep feeding on seaweed and a little thin grass that occasionally grows outside the wall. Walk on to Strom Ness Point and then through a gate in the sheep dyke to see the Broch of Burrian, part of an extensive Iron Age settlement. The tower, the centre piece of the settlement, was excavated in the 1880s. It was occupied into the Pictish period, 800AD or later. Christian objects were found including the Burrian Cross inscribed on a piece of flat stone. This has been adopted as a motif in modern Orcadian jewellery.

4 Walk on along the rough shore, close to the sheep dyke, as quietly as you can, if in July and August, to avoid disturbing the seal colony with its many young. Then take the gate leading from the beach, just beyond the fishermen's tall cairn. Beyond, walk the walled track. To the right stands part of an old turf and stone dyke called Muckle Gersty. It is one of two that divided the island into three and both could be pre-Norse. Legend has it that they were erected by three brothers who used them to apportion the island.

5 Stroll on to pass, on the right, a disused meal mill with two old millstones against a wall. This was provided by Mr Trail, the laird in 1907, and was used for grinding corn. Continue along the lane. At the crossroads you may have to make a decision. If you have spent too much time on the sands, then walk ahead to return to the airfield. But if you still have a couple of hours to spare, turn right to pass the post office and Burrian Inn.

6 At the next road junction (at the war memorial) bear right and stride the long narrow road which, after three-quarters of a mile,

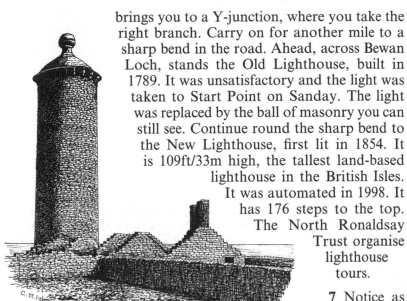
Old Lighthouse

brings you to a Y-junction, where you take the right branch. Carry on for another mile to a sharp bend in the road. Ahead, across Bewan Loch, stands the Old Lighthouse, built in 1789. It was unsatisfactory and the light was taken to Start Point on Sanday. The light was replaced by the ball of masonry you can still see. Continue round the sharp bend to the New Lighthouse, first lit in 1854. It is 109ft/33m high, the tallest land-based lighthouse in the British Isles. It was automated in 1998. It has 176 steps to the top. The North Ronaldsay Trust organise lighthouse tours.

7 Notice as you walk the square walled enclosures known as punds used for dipping and clipping sheep. Look too for the circular enclosures, called plantiecrues, in which seeds were planted, mostly kale. When the plants were strong enough they were planted out. Each croft had its own enclosure. Then return by the same route to the airport. If time is short someone will offer you a lift. No one in a vehicle seems to ignore anyone on foot, one of the pleasant things that make North Ronaldsay special.

Practicals

Type of walk: A great experience to visit this remote island. Spend your time walking both the beach and the very quiet roads. Or you might be tempted to see if you can manage the 13–mile walk outside the spectacular wall.

Distance: 9 miles/14.5km
Time: 6 hours
Maps: OS Explorer 465 / Landranger 5

35

Doun Helzie, Sanday

Park by the electricity sub-station, which is on your left, grid ref 612358. To access this, drive along the only road from the pier, B9070, for two miles and soon after it winds right, take the next right turn onto the old road that leads, in less than a mile, to the parking layby, just before the few houses at Stove. The Orkney Islands Shipping Company's ferry leaves Kirkwall pier and takes about two hours to reach the deep-water pier at Loth.

In 1973 a **submarine cable** was installed bringing electricity for Sanday from Stronsay. More cables go from Sanday to Eday and North Ronaldsay. These two sparsely populated islands use very little power (less than 1 megawatt). Sanday's two wind turbines, installed in 2004, produce more power (2.5 megawatts each) than the island needs and now there is a net export of power from the island.

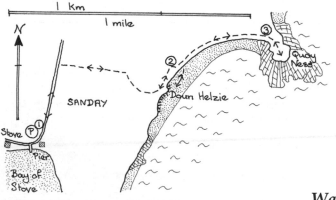

Walk 35

1 Walk back along the narrow lane to take a sandy track going off right. At the gate across the track, turn right to walk with a wall to your left and a wire fence to your right. At the next corner bear left and go on a grassy way still with the wall to your right and newer fencing to your left. At the end of the grassy way continue on along a narrow path, over rough grassy dunes, until you come parallel with the yellow diamond-shaped board, where electricity comes ashore through the submarine cable.

Cliff, Doun Helzie

2 Here look for the start of a narrow trod, dropping slightly left, down the dunes to the shore. Turn right and, if the tide permits, walk towards the fascinating cliffs of Doun Helzie. Look for caves, a natural arch, and the unusual texture of the cliffs. This is a place where you will want to linger. Then stroll back along the lovely sands, looking for otter tracks, haul-out tracks of seals and unusual shells as you go. Out on the skerries

Otter

137

at the far end of the bay you might spot a dozen seals or more. Continue on along the sands towards Quoyness.

3 Here look for the unusual sandstone dyke that stretches out to sea, which has been carved by the sea and wind into beautifully regular slabs. Then climb up the now shallow dunes by a narrow path to walk on to Quoy Ness. After a pleasing pause here return to the parking area by your outward route. Look across from here to the ruins of a 19th century 'model farm', with boiler house, red brick chimney and steam engine room. Do not visit.

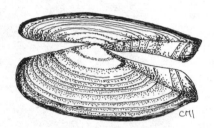

Faroe Sunset Shell

Practicals

Type of walk: Short but on a good day this is a glorious beach to explore.

Distance: 2 miles/3.4km
Time: 1–2 hours
Maps: OS Explorer 465 / Landranger 5

NB Take care along the fenced grassy trods at the start of the walk, where at the time of writing a considerable amount of old wire, some barbed, has been left on the track. The vegetation has now grown through it and it is very easy to trip. One stretch can be tiresome because of nettles.

36

Backaskaill Bay, Sanday

Park on the left of the reinforced track just after ruined Cross Kirk, grid ref 652393. To reach the parking area drive nine miles along the B9070, then turn right along the B9068 to Kettletoft, a picturesque village and harbour where the ferry used to call. It is well worth a visit. From Kettletoft return along the road to take the reinforced track that leads off, left, beyond the last building of How farm on the edge of the village. For access by ferry see walk 35.

On your **ferry journey** you can see Shapinsay with its grand Balfour Castle, and much of Mainland of Orkney, Rousay with its high hills, Hoy with its even higher hills often in mist, and Wyre and Egilsay, both green and low-lying. The ferry may call at Eday. Stronsay lies just across the sound.

Ferry, Sanday

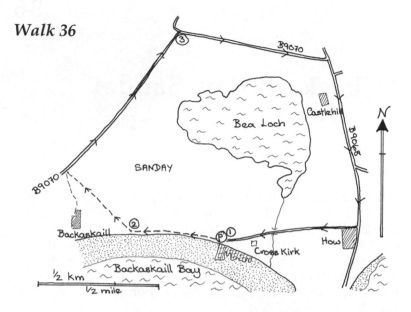

Walk 36

Cross Kirk dates from the 16th century. It is believed that the ruins stand on the site of a Viking settlement. It has been ruinous for a long time so take care near the building. The graveyard is surrounded by a high stone wall and here the Sanday folklorist, Walter Traill Dennison is buried. In summer look for the extensive patches of pink and mauve eyebright and the delicate heartsease surrounding the gravestones. In December 1994 there was a fatal stranding of eleven sperm whales on the beach just below the graveyard.

1 From the graveyard, continue along the track. Beyond the barrier, follow a narrow sandy path through the marram grass stabilising the dunes to a wide steepish track leading to the white sands of Backaskaill Bay.

Pansies

140

Turn right and dawdle along the glorious shore, where you might see seals. Look also for the colourful Faroese sunset shells, wavey hatchet shells and long razor shells, locally called 'spoots'. After walking for nearly half a mile, look for a gap in the dunes, on your right, 200yds before Backaskaill farm.

Golden Plover

2 Climb the fenced way to the metal gate. Beyond, pass the picnic area and walk the steadily ascending track. To the right, across the pasture, lies Bea Loch, a placid sheet of water, very attractive to a variety of birds. Pass through another gate and walk to the B-road, which comes from the ferry, where you turn right. As you stroll on, look for the very large flagstones used for roofing cottages and outhouses, and enjoy the view of the loch below in its shallow grassy depression.

3 Follow the road as it bears right and continue to the T-junction where you turn right again. As you near How farm turn right to walk the track to rejoin your car just beyond the ruined church.

Practicals

Type of walk: A delightful circular walk along the shore and quiet rural roads.

Distance: 3½ miles/5.5km
Time: 2 hours
Maps: OS Explorer 465 / Landranger 5

37

Quoyness chambered cairn from Lady Village, Sanday

Park on the hard standing next to the fire station just after passing the war memorial, grid ref 687410. To access this, take the B9070 from the ferry for 6½ miles. Turn right onto the B9068 and, almost immediately, turn left. At the T-junction drive, right, into Lady village. For details of access to the island by ferry see walk 35.

Quoyness communal tomb dates from about 3000 BC, and is similar to Maeshowe on Mainland Orkney. Two carved stones and a bone pin resemble finds at Skara Brae. The remains of at least ten adults and four or five children were found in pits beneath the floor. Tombs such as this were used by many generations. The glass roof is modern, but the stonework of the main chamber stands to its original height of 13ft. The entrance to the impressive rectangular chamber is low and narrow (2ft high) and

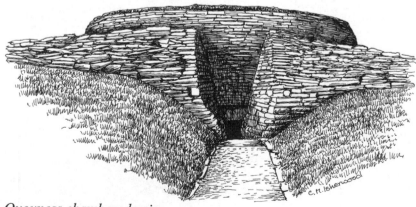

Quoyness chambered cairn

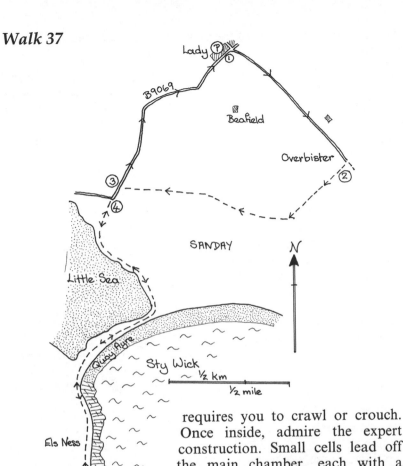

Lady

B9069

Beafield

Overbister

③

④

SANDAY

N

Little Sea

Quoy Ayre

Sty Wick

~ ½ km

½ mile

Els Ness

⑤ Quoyness
Chambered
Cairn

requires you to crawl or crouch. Once inside, admire the expert construction. Small cells lead off the main chamber, each with a sturdy lintel. The cells are shaped like beehives. Again some crawling is required to see these.

1 Return to the war memorial and take the narrow road that goes off directly opposite. As you carry on, look right to see the farm of Beafield, which stands on a mound, composed of man-made materials, indicative of the antiquity of a settlement here.

2 When the road ceases to be metalled, turn right to walk a delightful grassy trod. Ignore the track going off right to a dwelling called Bu (farm), with its green box for the post. Carry on along the way to where the path divides. Here take the right fork. Pass

South Lodge, once part of the Geramount estate, and stroll on to the B9069.

3 Turn left and, at the corner where the 'main' road curves right, walk along it for a hundred yards to see the ruined roofless shell of Lady Kirk. Here you may wish to enter the graveyard and climb the steps, on the outside wall, to the top, to see the 'devil's clawmarks' on a stone, part of the balustrade. Return to the corner and follow the signpost directions for 'Quoyness Chambered Cairn' to walk, right, along a narrow track.

4 The way soon becomes an impacted sandy track as it swings left along the side of the Little Sea, an area of tidal sand flats. Follow the winding track as it becomes grassy, with Sty Wick Bay to your left. Here you might spot seals lazing on the skerries. Pause as you go to look back to see the magnificent curve of the bay. Then pass through two gates as you continue on a much rougher track for three-quarters of a mile to come to the splendid chambered tomb.

Grey seal

5 Return along your outward route to reach the 'main road' at the bend. Turn right. Pass an area partly surrounded by high wire fencing, the island's rubbish tip. Here the refuse is bagged and sent to the Mainland by ferry! Continue on to see the gaunt roofless house, on your right. This was the well proportioned late-Georgian house of Geramount. Carry on to rejoin your vehicle.

Practicals

Type of walk: A delightful walk with lots of interest along the way.

Distance: 2¾ miles/4.5km
Time: 2 hours
Maps: OS Explorer 465 / Landranger 5

38

Holms of Ire, Sanday

Park alongside Burness kirkyard, grid ref 671449. To access this, leave Loth pier by the B9070 and drive for nearly six miles to the junction with the B9068. Turn left and after three more miles park by the cemetery. See walk 35 for details on getting to Sanday.

The Holms of Ire are only accessible at low tide. In summer the inner holm is colourful with sea thrift, pink and white campion, and on the boulders at the top of the beach the translucent blue oyster plant thrives. The outer holm provides nesting sites for great black-backed gulls, black guillemots and arctic terns. It is also where numerous common seals haul out for their annual moult.

Model yacht races take place on **Roos Loch**. Handmade wooden sailboats are sent across the loch and then coaxed through 'gates' set up by the umpire.

Oyster plant

1 Head on along the continuing road for a short way. To your left stands the imposing Scar house and its out-buildngs. Opposite, on your right, stands a tower on Mill Brae, believed to be the base of an old windmill. Carry on past, on your right, Orkney Angora, based in a charming white cottage, and walk on round right, on what has become a grassy track. Go on to cross a private piece of

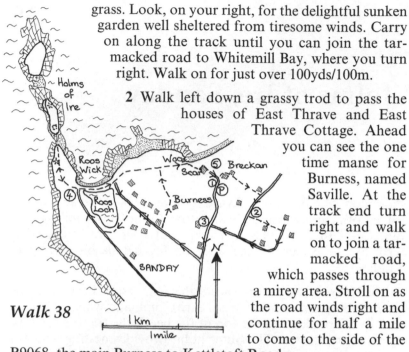

grass. Look, on your right, for the delightful sunken garden well sheltered from tiresome winds. Carry on along the track until you can join the tarmacked road to Whitemill Bay, where you turn right. Walk on for just over 100yds/100m.

2 Walk left down a grassy trod to pass the houses of East Thrave and East Thrave Cottage. Ahead you can see the one time manse for Burness, named Saville. At the track end turn right and walk on to join a tarmacked road, which passes through a mirey area. Stroll on as the road winds right and continue for half a mile to come to the side of the B9068, the main Burness to Kettletoft Road.

Walk 38

3 Turn left and head on for a quarter of a mile and, at the telephone box, turn right. Continue for three-quarters of a mile until you can take a track on the left. This winds round close to Roos Loch and joins a metalled road at Bellevue. Carry on, right, with the loch beside you to the right. At the end of the road stride on along the continuing track towards the two holms. These are separated by the Inner Sound and the Outer Sound, which can only be crossed at low tide (check tide tables).

4 After your explorations, return to the 'end' of the metalled road and turn left to walk the path along the shingle bank separating Roos Loch from the bay, Roos Wick. This bank is popular with otters. At the end of the path, join the metalled road and walk right to pass Roos Loch, again on your right. Continue for just over half a mile and then take the track going off left. Go past West Thrave and then follow the grassy way as it bears sharp left. Stroll on to a junction of tracks, where you turn right to walk to Woo. Pass a pretty dwelling on the left and the remains of a

146

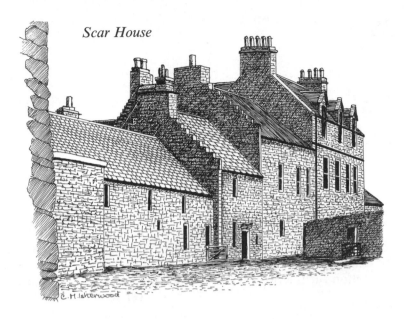

Scar House

watermill to your right. Beyond, go with the track as it turns sharp right and brings you to Scar, the impressive 19th century house and outbuildings. Cross the farmyard and turn left round more buildings. Then bear right, but first peep over the gate, now on your left, to see the magnificent proportions of the house itself.

5 The path now becomes metalled and ascends to join the Burness-Kettletoft road. Walk right to where you have parked by the cemetery.

Practicals

Type of walk: An excellent ramble. The grassy tracks are a delight to walk and the loch, the holms and the shingle bank a joy on a good day.

Distance:	5¼ miles/8.5km. Add on the distance covered on the holms.
Time:	3 hours
Maps:	OS Explorer 465 / Landranger 5

39

Vat of Kirbister and Odin Bay, Stronsay

Park in the small parking area above Odin Bay, grid ref 683242. To reach Stronsay, take the roll-on roll-off ferry from Kirkwall. This takes just over 1½ hours to reach Whitehall pier. To access the parking area, leave the pier by the B9060 and, at the T-junction turn, left onto the B9062. Just after a mile, turn left and follow the narrower road for nearly 1½ miles, ignoring the first left turn and taking the second. After a quarter of a mile, turn right and continue to the signposted layby.

Whitehall village takes its name from a 17th century house built here by Patrick Fea an ex-privateer. The village and the splendid harbour are monuments to the herring boom of the early 19th century. Then the industry employed hundreds of men, women and children. The old Stronsay fish market has been renovated and features an interpretation centre, café facilities and hostel.

Walk 39

Vat of Kirbister

The wind and the sea have shaped the coast of Stronsay over the millennia bringing about the amazing scenery of stacks, geos, coves, sheer cliffs and the **Vat of Kirbister**. All of these make this a spectacular walk. The Vat is a natural, partially collapsed sea cave (a gloup) with part of the roof remaining, forming a spectacular arch that spans the entrance. Sea stacks such as the **Tam's Castle**, are formed when the middle of an arch collapses, leaving a free standing pillar of rock. On the summit of Tam's Castle are the remains of an early Christian hermitage. Monks became hermits and lived apart from society for long periods of time on

149

several of Stronsay's stacks. A geo is a narrow sea inlet into the cliffs, which is often very deep, very long and with steep sides. Wide geos provided somewhere that locals could launch a fishing boat. The erosion of the cliffs provides good nesting ledges for birds.

1 From the parking area pass through the 'barrier' gate and walk the wide fenced grassy track that leads to the cliff edge. Turn right to start your walk round Odin Bay. All the small streams that hurtle towards the sea are crossed by wooden 'bridges'. Then the walk continues outside the fence and you should continue circumspectly along the very high cliffs. Carry on until you come to the Vat, where you will want to use your camera.

2 Head on along the cliff path to see Tam's Castle (sea stack). Then go on along the magnificently sculptured coastline, past stacks, geos, arches and ledges where, in summer, hundreds of fulmars and kittiwakes nest. Inland stretch wide pastures and again, in summer, these resound with the calls of curlews. Walk on to wind round Burgh Head, an area of northern maritime heath where shrubby heather, bell heather, crowberry and creeping willow have developed a springy carpet. Look across to The Brough (a stack) where you can see the remains of a wall, part of the largest of Stronsay's hermitage sites. When it was occupied there would have been a rock bridge.

Kittiwakes

3 Stroll on along the dramatic coast winding round geos. Keep outside the fence to come to a stile. Beyond, wind left to climb onto Lamb Head, which is dotted with archeaological sites. Beyond the Head the high cliffs are replaced by a gentler rocky shore where, after nearly a mile, you reach a cattle grid, and a concrete road used by vehicles to reach the shore.

4 Walk this road and, where it becomes tarmacked, wind right and carry on to crossroads and the old schoolroom, nearly a mile from the shore. Ignore the B9060 and carry on ahead for a mile and a quarter to where you can turn right. Stride on for a quarter of a mile and then turn right again to walk half a mile to where you have parked.

Creeping Willow

Practicals

Type of walk: The way round the coastline is not to be missed. There is almost three miles of road walking. But Stronsay's roads are very quiet, straight, fenced and give fine views across the well tended fields.

Distance: 6½ miles/10.4km
Time: 3–4 hours
Maps: OS Explorer 465 / Landranger 5

40

Rothiesholm, Stronsay

Park in a small car park near the east end of the Sand of Rothiesholm, grid ref 643249. To access this leave Whitehall village by the B9060. Turn left onto the B9062 and drive for a mile to turn right onto the B9061, signposted Rothiesholm, and go on for just under a mile. Turn left opposite to the Loch of Matpow onto a wide fenced clinker track to park in a small sandy area. (See walk 39 for details on access to the island).

The island of **Stronsay** is about seven miles long from north to south. Its odd shape has been described as 'all arms and legs' because of the three large bays that cut into the land. Burgh Hill

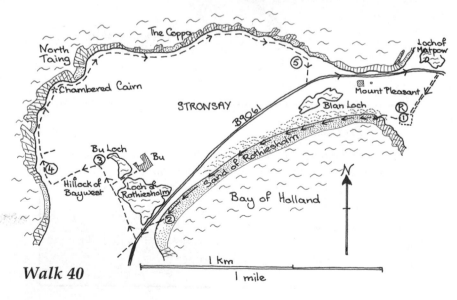

Walk 40

is the highest point, at 154 ft/46m above sea level, on this low-lying island.

During the heyday of **Whitehall village** the harbour's skyline was dominated with the masts of up to 300 boats of the herring fleet. Tales are told that on a Sunday it was occasionally possible to walk to Papa Stronsay across the decks of the anchored fleet.

1 Go through the barrier gate and follow the yellow arrow directing you ahead, through sand dunes, onto the shore of the wonderful Sand of Rothiesholm, with the turquoise-blue water turning to purple as it recedes over seaweed. Turn right and walk the lovely sands. As you go look for various interesting shells including the very rare canoe shell. This is the only beach in Orkney where you can find it. If the tide is too high you can walk behind the shallow dunes. Continue on until the sand is replaced by wave-rounded stones.

2 Here, climb onto the banking. Look across to the road and head on to a stile. Beyond, walk left along the road and, in a few steps, take the arrowed stile on your right. Walk on along a rough indistinct path with the Loch of Rothiesholm to your right, where you might spot shelduck. Cross two stretches of

Arctic skua

duckboarding, keeping to the left of the loch and carry on past Bu Loch, where you might see, in summer, arctic skuas bathing. In autumn these lochs are havens for migrating waders.

3 Continue on, with care over the mirey ground, to reach an arrowed post, directing you diagonally across a pasture, on a rather wet path, to reach another arrowed post on a hillock. This is the Hillock of Baywest, an excavated mound containing a burial chamber dating from 3000BC. To the north is a mound, which contains a broch, the broad platform extending from one side conceals the collapsed remains of an extensive Iron Age village. Beyond step through another small wet area to cross two more board walks and then head on to a stile. Beyond, follow the arrow on a post, directing you right.

4 Walk on along a long stretch of more gentle coast, with a derelict wall of seashore boulders to your left. Ignore the farmer's first track, going off right. Continue on along the lovely way with, below, wide plates of rock and rugged skerries stretching out into the sea, trapping long strands of tangle as the tide recedes. Go on past Ver Geo and North Taing and then The Coppa. Eventually the way bends round right, with St Catherine's Bay stretching away to your left.

5 When your way is barred by a gate, turn right to walk a wide grassy fenced track, which leads you to the B-road. The loch opposite is generally only there in the winter, when it plays host to pintail ducks. Turn left and walk a short way and then, opposite the Loch of Matpow, turn right onto the clinker track and walk to the parking place, on your left.

Pintail

Practicals

Type of walk: A beautiful sandy beach to stroll along and then a low rocky coastline, with views across to Eday. Very peaceful.

Distance: 3½ miles/5.7km
Time: 2 hours
Maps: OS Explorer 465 / Landranger 5

Clan Walks

A series of walks described by Mary Welsh, covering some of the most popular holiday areas in the Scottish Highlands and Islands.

Titles published so far include:

1. 44 WALKS ON THE ISLE OF ARRAN
2. WALKING THE ISLE OF SKYE
3. WALKING WESTER ROSS
4. WALKS IN PERTHSHIRE
5. WALKING THE WESTERN ISLES
6. WALKING ORKNEY
7. WALKING SHETLAND
8. WALKING THE ISLES OF ISLAY, JURA AND COLONSAY
9. WALKS ON CANNA, RUM, EIGG AND MUCK
10. WALKS ON TIREE, COLL, COLONSAY AND A TASTE OF MULL
11. WALKING DUMFRIES AND GALLOWAY
12. WALKING ARGYLL AND BUTE
13. WALKING DEESIDE, DONSIDE AND ANGUS
14. WALKING THE TROSSACHS, LOCH LOMONDSIDE AND THE CAMPSIE FELLS
15. WALKING GLENCOE, LOCHABER AND THE GREAT GLEN

OTHER TITLES IN PREPARATION

Books in this series can be ordered through booksellers anywhere. In the event of difficulty write to
Clan Books, The Cross, DOUNE, FK16 6BE, Scotland.